LOVIN _ . .JAIN

After a Spouse Has Died

Loving Again:
After a Spouse Has Died

W. Bruce Conway - Book Design
Friday Harbor, Washington
www.wbconway.com

Betty Reynolds, Cover Illustration
Orcas Island, Washington

Dedication

To lovers everywhere. Loving is always a leap of faith. A leap with no guarantees—no one knows what the future holds. Love breaks our hearts and lifts us to the highest heights. It entices us all to dance with its power and tenderness.

Acknowledgements

The stories found on these pages have come to light only because a group of courageous individuals were willing to place their trust in my husband Alan and me and told their stories. They were generous with their time, their thoughts and their feelings. They were willing to revisit painful and stressful events and times in their lives. They were willing to reveal sensitive personal and family issues. They gladly shared their joys. It is difficult to express in words the magnitude of our gratitude to them. Thank you each one! I hope I have accurately portrayed your thoughts and feelings.

Any writer, like any Oscar Award winning actor, feels the significance of all the people and forces that stand behind and alongside him or her. I feel that now as I contemplate all the people who supported my efforts to bring this project to the printed page. My friend, River Malcolm, was my earliest source of encouragement and was there still at the end. There were many readers along the way who offered welcomed advice and suggestions—Kathryn Bowes, Jim Connell, Virginia Erhardt, Andrea Groberg, Lory Jenkins, Mary Nash, Rachel Newcombe, Jeanne Olmsted, Greg Papanikolas, Vicki Weber, Esther Wender. My sincere thanks. If I overlooked you, I apologize and please let me know. Others really took me to task and substantially altered the text—Donna Evans-Deyermond, Mary Anne

Owen, and Marilyn McGuire. Thanks to all you gave and contributed.

In the search for publication, an arena in which I was a complete novice, Cynthia Frank and Joe Shaw from Cypress Press were my first professional contacts and provided sensitive and needed support and services. Additional thanks to Marilyn McGuire for connecting me to them. Maria August and Lorna Rhodes helped in crafting proposals to submit to prospective agents when I really needed their expertise. Although that route proved to be unsuccessful, I do thank the very busy agents who took the time to respond to queries beyond a form rejection. It meant a lot to me as I tried to navigate in a world that was foreign and intimidating.

To Milly Vetterlein who led me to W. Bruce Conway, my book designer, a big bow! What a productive lunch together that turned out to be. He has been so welcoming and talented—a computer wizard. He made it happen. To my friend Betty Reynolds, whose artistic talents grace the cover, I am deeply grateful and indebted.

Finally, to Alan, who came along on this ride even though it was not a place of ease or comfort for him. He will downplay his contribution to the interviewing process and to the editing he did of the writing, but his contribution was incredibly valuable. As a widower himself, he had a perspective that I lacked. His calm and kind manner unquestionably contributed to a sense of emotional safety that set our couples at ease. Thanks for taking another leap with me!

LOVING AGAIN

After a Spouse Has Died

Janice Sargent Wiemeyer, Ph.D.

W.B. Conway
Book Design
Friday Harbor, Washington

Table of Contents

Introduction

This book was conceived while Alan and I were on a camping trip in 1996. We would marry the following year. The trip was part of our getting to know one another. The year before, Alan's wife of twenty-four years had died of metastasized breast cancer. I had ended a six-year relationship with another man. Though Alan and I had known each other at a distance for several years, we had not had a real conversation until six months before the trip. We'd been guests at Thanksgiving dinner at the home of his nephew who is married to one of my best friends. I referred to Alan then as "Uncle Alan." We enjoyed lively conversation and went to the symphony together the following night. Then he returned to Washington State where he lived; I lived in Utah.

We saw each other again almost every day at Christmastime and began our tentative journey into a relationship. Many phone calls and trips to visit one another whenever feasible strengthened our connection. We were having a wonderful time discovering each other and being together, often feeling like teenagers again, but all was not blissful. Alan was not sure how he felt about me. He expected to feel the same way he'd felt about his wife, but he didn't—he felt differently. Members of his family were struggling with our being together. I was struggling with being drawn to him even though there were difficulties already.

As a psychologist I was accustomed to consulting literature for information. I scoured bookstores and libraries looking for some guidance or understanding about the challenges we were encountering. Certainly other couples had preceded us on this path. While there were scores of books about grieving and mourning and loss, there was virtually nothing about how a widow or widower might approach finding a new partner, or about the challenges that could beset such a journey. In the books about grief, a paragraph or two were embedded here and there suggesting a person might eventually want to socialize again, but no significant discussions of the situation Alan and I found ourselves in.

So, there on a small road in rural Colorado, while talking about the challenges we were facing, we decided to write the book we were looking for. We envisioned interviewing couples who had found loving relationships after the death of a spouse. Alan had personal experience of losing a wife through death, and I had experience interviewing and talking with people about their lives. We seemed well suited for the project. As Alan drove along, I took notes about the topics we wanted to cover and outlined chapters and details.

After constructing a semi-structured interview, in 2005 we began interviewing people. Our last couple was interviewed in 2012. Alan and I did most face-to-face interviews together. I did the telephone interviews alone because having four people on a phone call was overly complicated. In 2012, on retreat in Mexico, I finally began writing about our experience and those of the people who consented to be a part of this project. To them, we owe immense gratitude. We asked much of them: to uncover memories they might have been keeping dormant; to share difficulties they had encountered in their own journeys; and to share their intimate feelings about finding new loves.

Of course, participants could choose not to respond to any one of our questions, but that rarely happened. People really opened their hearts to us and were glad to be a part of this endeavor. We wish that what we've learned from them and from our own experience will offer support and hope to individuals whose lives have changed forever due to the death of a spouse. Because our own experiences prompted this project, parts of our story are included in the chapters that follow. Names and other identifying information of all other couples have been altered so that the responses of the participants remain anonymous.

While Alan and I together conceived of this project, formulated the semi-structured interview, and conducted the face-to-face interviews, the writing is mine. Alan has read every word, and his keen mind, recommendations, and revisions are present throughout.

—Janice Sargent Wiemeyer, Ph.D., 2016

PARTICIPANTS*

Widows and widowers names
are in capital letters

ALAN. Alan was widowed at age fifty-four, after twenty-five years of marriage. He and Janice (the author) have been married for fifteen years.

ANN AND BRAD. Ann was widowed at age fifty-three after twenty-two years of marriage. She had an adolescent daughter and son just out of high school at the time of her husband's death. Brad was widowed at age forty-six after ten years of marriage. He had a nine year old son and an adolescent step-daughter at home at the time of his wife's death. Ann and Brad have been together for two years.

BETTY AND REX. Betty was widowed at age fifty-seven after thirty-five years of marriage. Rex was widowed at age sixty-nine after twenty-one years of marriage. They have been together for a total of thirteen years, married for twelve years.

BILL. Bill was widowed at age sixty-six after thirty-nine years of marriage. He and Kate have been together a total of two years, married for one.

BONNIE. Bonnie was widowed at age twenty-six after eighteen months of marriage. She had a one month old baby at the time. She and Peter have been married for forty-one years.

CYNTHIA. Cynthia was widowed at age sixty-six after thirty-eight years of marriage. She and Scott have been together for just over two years.

CAROL. Carol was widowed at age thirty-five after seven years of marriage. She and Andrew have been together a total of fifteen years, married for ten years.

CORNELIA AND DOUG. Cornelia's lesbian partner died when Cornelia was sixty-five after fifteen years together. Doug was widowed at age seventy after twenty-four years of marriage. They have been together for almost one year and are engaged to be married.

ELEANOR. Eleanor was widowed at age fifty-eight after thirty years of marriage. She and Brandon have been together for five and a half years.

ELLA. Ella was widowed at age sixty-four after thirty-five years of marriage. She and Hank have been together for almost two years and are engaged to be married.

FRANK. Frank was widowed at age fifty-nine after thirty-five years of marriage. He remarried three years later. Information obtained from personal communication, not interviewed.

GEORGE AND MARIANNE. George was widowed at age sixty-four after thirty-six years of marriage. Marianne was widowed at age fifty-six after twenty-seven years of marriage. They have been together for a total of ten years, married for nine years.

HANNAH AND JOHN. Hannah was widowed at age fifty-four after thirty-four years of marriage. John was widowed at age sixty-nine after fifty years of marriage. They have been together a total of eleven years, married for ten years.

HELEN. Helen's lesbian partner died when Helen was thirty-eight years old after being together for four years. She and Nancy have been together for eight years.

JOE. Joe was widowed at age fifty-five after thirty-five years of marriage. He and Marion have been together for ten years, married for eight years.

LARRY. Larry was widowed at age forty-one after eight years of marriage. His daughters were two and five years old when their mother died. He and Barbara have been married for thirteen years. Larry declined to be interviewed.

LAURA. Laura was widowed at age forty-seven after ten years of marriage, when her daughter was seven years old. She and Brian have been together for seven years, married for five years.

LORRAINE AND PATRICK. Lorraine was widowed at age seventy-six and Patrick at age eighty, each after fifty-seven years of marriage. They have been together a total of six years, married for five years.

MARIA. Maria was widowed at age thirty-four after seven years of marriage, when her daughter was almost two years old. She and Nate had been married for twenty years but were separated and anticipating divorce.

MARILYN AND STUART. Marilyn was widowed at age sixty-five after twenty-three years of marriage. Stuart was widowed at age sixty-three after thirty years of marriage. They have been together for six years.

MILTON. Milton was widowed at age fifty-two after twenty-seven years of marriage. He and Margaret have been together for fifteen years, married for thirteen years.

PEGGY. Peggy was widowed at age sixty after thirty years of marriage. She and Kirk have been together for just over one year.

RACHEL. Rachel was widowed at age forty-nine after twenty two years of marriage in a heterosexual relationship. She and Mira have been together for almost three years.

ROBERT. Robert is a personal friend who was widowed at age sixty-two after twenty-nine years of marriage. He has not remarried.

SANDRA. Sandra was widowed at age sixty after forty years of marriage. She and Paul have been together for two years, married for one and a half years.

SHARON. Sharon was widowed at age sixty-seven after thirty years of marriage. Her current husband who was widowed at age seventy-nine after fifty years of marriage declined to be interviewed. They have been together for a total of three years, married for two years.

TOM. Tom was widowed at age sixty-four after forty-six years of marriage. He and Sally have been together for three years and married for one year.

TONY. Tony was widowed at age seventy-four after twenty-seven years of marriage. He and Jody have been together for four years.

TRENT. Trent was widowed at age thirty-three after nine years of marriage. He and Diane were together for seven years, married for three years, and divorced.

TRINA. Trina was widowed at age fifty after twenty-nine years of marriage. She and Mike have been together for eight years.

*Names are fictitious to protect anonymity of participants, except for the author and her husband Alan.

Chapter 1

The Stories and the People

It has been six years since Mary's death, and still, on some Sundays her absence brings a sadness that hurts in my chest. I don't understand how this can be. I am remarried, I love my wife, and our life together is good.

—Frank

Alan's memories of Susan, once crushing for him, are now sweet and bring him pleasure. Cynthia, who had a very troubled relationship with her deceased husband, is happy to keep her memories of him far from her new life with Scott. Frank's, Alan's, and Cynthia's experiences illustrate the ongoing emotions that can characterize the death of a spouse and the building of a new loving, intimate relationship.

Close to one million people are widowed every year in the United States. Each of them must grieve the loss and, at some time, decide whether to consider loving a partner again. Confronting this decision can be confusing and distressing as well as wonderful and exhilarating. Many factors color the process of moving into new relationships, such as the nature of the relationship with the deceased spouse, attitudes and support of family members and friends, and one's willingness to risk tender feelings again.

This book recounts how the people we talked with navigated this complex territory. Each made the decision to open his or her heart and life to love again. When interviewed, all but two of the participants were still with their new partners. In the following pages, we will consider many aspects of their stories: the quality of their previous relationships; the cause of their partners' deaths; their grief; the process of considering new relationships; the place of the deceased in new relationships; reactions of friends and family; challenges encountered and strategies for problem solving; factors that encouraged and solidified new relationships; and surprises people found on this journey.

The people we interviewed were either known to us, referred to us by others who knew about our project, or referred by other participants. There was no intent or attempt at a random sample. Couples were defined as a pair who considered themselves partnered, whether married or not. At least one of the pair had experienced the death of a spouse or partner earlier in life. We interviewed twenty-four couples, including ourselves; two people (one widowed, one a partner) whose spouses declined participation; and one widower and one widow who were no longer with their new spouses. Following are more facts about the group at the time of each interview.

Relationships

In eight of the couples, both individuals had earlier experienced the death of a spouse or partner.

Two couples were lesbians. A woman in one of these couples had previously been in a heterosexual relationship.

One woman in a heterosexual relationship had previously been in a lesbian relationship.

Ages of the Women

The ages of the women when interviewed ranged from twenty-seven years to eighty-three years, with an average of sixty-one years. The woman aged twenty-seven was atypical, as the next nearest woman in age was forty-six.

The ages of the men when interviewed ranged from forty-five years to eighty-six years, with an average of sixty-eight years.

The average age when widowed was fifty-six years.

Previous Relationships

Thirty-six individuals had experienced the death of a spouse or partner: twenty women and sixteen men.

Duration of earlier relationships ranged from one and a half years to fifty-seven years with an average of twenty-seven and a half years.

Current Relationships

Duration ranged from one and a half years to forty-two years, an average of seven and a half years.

Participants were therefore generally older individuals who had been in long-term relationships prior to a spouse or partner dying. Our couples had a higher level of education than the general population of the United States and were financially stable. The majority of the couples lived in Washington State, but we also interviewed people in Utah, California, Minnesota, Arizona, and the United Kingdom.

In the course of interviewing, we discovered that the reactions of participants' children to new loves were particularly challenging. This was certainly true for Alan and me. Therefore, we asked several people if we could speak with their children to learn directly from them what their experiences had been. All the children we approached consented—one teenager and four adult children.

In the pages that follow, words spoken by those we interviewed are often indented. Because we did not tape the interviews, the indented words are usually a compilation of the person's ideas or expressions; if they are a direct quote, quotation marks so indicate. The words *spouse* and *partner* are used interchangeably to indicate that there was a couple, either married or not.

Chapter 2

Previous Relationships

Bruce and I were married for thirty-five years. We were actually closer at the end of the relationship than at the beginning. We worked on our problems together and had a wonderful marriage.

—Eleanor

A few people who spoke with us had experienced the death of a spouse at a fairly young age, but most of our widows and widowers were older and had been in relationships for many years. Generally, this group mirrors widows and widowers, as being widowed becomes more likely as we age. Because women tend to outlive men, it's also true that as we age, more women are widowed than men.

Quality of Former Relationships

As would be expected, the quality of our participants' past relationships varied, but the vast majority were described as excellent or very good. Tom described his relationship with Christine in these words:

We were married for over forty years and had a very good marriage. We had a lot in common.

It felt "natural" to be married to Christine. We had similar goals, and assumed traditional roles in our life together.

Bill talked about his close relationship with his deceased wife Alexis:

We enjoyed the freedom afforded us as a couple without children, traveling to other countries and deriving satisfaction from our individual careers. We shared household responsibilities. I felt really fulfilled in that relationship.

Several individuals talked about their previous relationships in terms that suggested they were so deeply in love and interdependent they were almost "fused." For example, Joe told us:

Alice and I had been childhood sweethearts, together since our teens. We faced developmental issues together, had disagreements but worked them out, saw things in a similar way, and grew into adulthood as "a unit."

Though there is a tendency to idealize people after their deaths, the words and tone of these positive descriptions of past relationships rang true to us. New partners told us that being with someone whose earlier relationship had been a satisfying one was a positive factor for being in a relationship with them now.

Not all participants, however, described life with their deceased partners in positive terms. Karen felt that her first marriage to Alden had been good, but she'd had to make many compromises. This was echoed by Laura who felt she had suppressed parts of herself in her marriage to Jay because of his strong personality. Several women had to manage homes and children on their own, often due to their husbands' work demands. Others told of a lack of emotional intimacy or of contemplating divorce.

A few prior relationships were described as seriously troubled. John described how Louise's alcoholism had colored many years of their long relationship, and the frustrations he felt being unable to help her turn her life around. Cynthia described a similar pattern with Craig:

> *He struggled with alcoholism but was also self-centered and a big spender. He often left us in financial crises. Living with him was very stressful, and I considered leaving many times before he died in an accident.*

Though Carol had loved Peter and worked hard to make a good marriage, his perfectionism and emotional reactivity were major detractions from a peaceful life together. Emotional abuse, combined with illness, characterized the earlier lives of both Helen and Cornelia, each of whom had a partner who became very difficult as death approached, though the relationships had earlier been good.

Among the people who spoke with us, moving on to a new loving relationship was not directly correlated with the quality of the previous relationship in which a partner died. Individuals in partnerships from all points on the continuum, from earlier fulfilling relationships to highly troubled ones, had chosen to love after a spouses death. It might be easier to understand how a person from a very close relationship would choose to love again than might a person from a troubled relationship. We will explore some of the reasons for these decisions later, but suffice it to say that having one unsatisfactory marital relationship does not always dissuade one from pursuing a loving relationship in the future.

Causes of Spousal Death

The majority of our participants' spouses died from prolonged illnesses and disabilities. These conditions influenced marital relationships, for good and bad, in ways that did not characterize relationships where deaths were sudden and unexpected.

Cancer was the most frequent cause of death; sixteen of the thirty-six deceased spouses had some form of cancer. Brain tumors, aneurysms, strokes, and dementia were responsible for six deaths. Another five individuals died in accidents. Two died of chronic neurological diseases, two from heart disease, and one each from alcoholism, unspecified illness, and suicide.

Declining health lasting more than five years had been a part of nine relationships. Surprisingly, several widows and widowers reported becoming closer emotionally to their ailing spouses as death approached, even though caretaking was often both a physical and emotional strain.

Laura said:

Jay and I had a sense of partnership in dealing with his illness and declining health that had been absent previously in our marriage due to our independent lives and Jay's strong personality. This unified focus brought us closer together, even though he was sick.

Similarly, Brad told us:

The relationship between Becky and me was filled with both good and tumultuous times, even talk of divorce. However, when Becky's illness became terminal, her own spiritual journey also transformed our relationship, and we were very close for many months before she died.

Eleanor found:

I struggled with accepting that Bruce's cancer was terminal, but once I'd accepted the unavoidable outcome, our time together was beautiful as we purposefully enjoyed all the time we could that remained.

In order to have time together with an ailing spouse, it was not unusual for people to report that they either quit work or decreased the amount of time they worked as their partners required more care or became more debilitated. The burden of caregiving for a partner whose health has been compromised can be overwhelming. Sharon's husband, Ben, had a progressive neurological disorder for most of their married life. As a career professional, Sharon was not only the primary breadwinner but also Ben's primary caregiver for many years. As he required increasingly more care Sharon became exhausted. Eventually she hired caretakers to give her some respite.

Ella, who had been Richard's primary caregiver, became anxious about the expanding medical aspects of his cancer care. She enlisted hospice for support for both of them. Hospice, friends, and family members were often named as invaluable sources of caretaking help. Healthy partners attempted to keep some balance in their lives and avoid being totally consumed by illness and caregiving.

Chapter 3

Grieving

When Linda died, the hardest part was the big hole of her absence. There was an empty space all around me, especially at home.

—Tony

The focus of our project was not the exploration of grief and grieving, but death and loss were an integral part of the lives of these widows and widowers. We did ask people, therefore, to tell us about reactions to their losses and about what they had found helpful as they grieved. As would be expected, individuals often mentioned more than one reaction. Almost half of the widows and widowers said they were either devastated or shocked by the loss of their partners, even though some of these deaths were expected. Alan said:

Though I knew that Susan was gravely ill and would die sometime soon and be released from her suffering, at the moment of her death I was struck by the absolute finality of her life and our life.

Hannah's husband, Fred, had a progressive neurological disorder and had been severely impaired for many years. Still, Hannah was shocked when he actually succumbed—that it was *that* moment.

Just over half of the individuals who talked with us related that after the death they felt a profound longing for their deceased partners. Maria described this as "deep loneliness." Sunday was mentioned as being the most difficult day of the week, and nighttime more difficult than daytime. This is understandable. Sundays and nighttimes are more likely to be when couples and families are together. Daytime and weekdays are often filled with work, school, and individual activities, but Sundays and evenings are for being together, times for sharing the events of busy lives, times for fun and pleasure.

Peggy told us:

It was hard being in the house alone without Stan. We had been like bookends—sharing equally in our lives, and now half of that life was gone. I will have that love in my heart forever, shining and joyful, and will take that love forward.

Many people missed being part of a relationship—experiencing the strangeness of being an individual, no longer an "us" or a "we." Even after the death of a long-term seriously compromised or ill spouse whose ability to relate had been minimal, the person left behind usually felt very lonely. Rachel reminded us that the structure of life changes when a partner is gone, regardless of the nature of the relationship. For those who had been heavily involved with caregiving an ill partner, death brought not only the loss of the person but also the loss of the caregiving role they had assumed. For example,

Lorraine told us:

> *I had purposely maintained some activities in addition to long-term care of Christopher, but after he died I realized how much time I had devoted to his care and the magnitude of the void now in my life.*

Her new husband, Patrick, a widower, experienced this void even more keenly:

> *After Elaine's death from a progressively debilitating illness, I felt lost. Not unlike many traditional marriages, Elaine had been the one to plan social, family, and other activities for us. My world narrowed a lot as Elaine's energy and capacity were depleted. When she died, the void was a deep chasm.*

Due to the effects of caregiving and the emotional toll of illness or the strains of a seriously troubled relationship, almost one third of the widowed reported a feeling of relief when their spouses died. For those with illness, the repeated hospitalizations, medical procedures and treatments, progressive lack of function, and pain were burdens not only for the sick but also for their partners as witnesses. Relief was almost always accompanied by deep sadness and sometimes guilt, creating what can be a complicated and confusing set of emotions. Feeling sad one moment, relieved the next, and then guilty can seem contradictory, incompatible, even crazy. Yet our feelings related to the death of someone very close to us are often mixed—just like our feelings when the person is alive. That is the nature of relationships.

In their book, *Liberating Losses: When Death Brings Relief,* grief counselor Jennifer Elison EdD, and author Chris McGonigle PhD, present in depth the complex nature of relief as a component of particular deaths. Their own experiences, combined with others', bring to light the often hidden feelings of relief that can accompany death. For example, a widow or widower might feel relief if he or she was married to an abusive person, or to a spouse with a long, painful or debilitating condition that required years of caregiving. Similarly, relief could follow the death of a partner with substance abuse issues, serious mental illness or dementia. Yet acknowledging relief after a death can feel taboo.

For those whose partners died unexpectedly, there was the element of shock. Maria, whose husband died in a sudden traumatic accident, said:

His death shattered my bubble of illusory safety. We live life in a state of illusion and can't contemplate all the dangers. Bad things happen, and when I walked into a room after his death, I carried that with me.

Trina, whose husband died suddenly of a heart attack, also expressed this vulnerability:

I felt afraid to look into the future—if his unforeseen death could happen, what other trauma could happen?

The belief we have that things will be "ordinary" is severely challenged when the "not so ordinary" occurs. In many ways, our culture doesn't prepare us well for the difficult things in life. Instead, the emphasis is on striving, happiness, hard work, and planning to ensure the good life. This leads us to expect that positive things should come our way, that the difficult things are somehow aberrant. When something bad happens, we often ask why me? rather than why not me? as if any of us is immune from *all* that life can bring.

Studies of Grieving

Poets, playwrights, philosophers, scientists, and many others have written about grief. Elisabeth Kübler-Ross, Swiss American psychiatrist, was one of the first to study people whose own death was approaching and describe what they experienced: denial, anger, bargaining, depression, and acceptance. This construct has been applied—erroneously, it could be argued—to the grief process that someone experiences *after* the death of a loved one. While all of the feelings Kübler-Ross recognized may be part of the process for a bereaved individual, they do not compose a reliable or consistent pattern.

In recent years, psychologist George Bonanno has embarked on a more rigorous study of bereaved individuals, expanding upon data gathered by a long-term survey, the "Changing Lives of Older Couples Study" (CLOC) from the University of Michigan, led by Camille Wortman (Carr, Nesse & Wortman, 2006). That survey began by collecting information from about 1,500 married people, couples in which the husband was at least sixty-five years old. When individuals died, the surviving spouses were asked to participate in follow-up interviews six, eighteen, and forty-eight months later. This study offered a unique opportunity to assess widows and widowers over time. The findings, which have surprised many, offer a fresh look at how people cope with loss, as described in Bonanno's book *The Other Side of Sadness: What the New Science of Bereavement Tells Us About Life After Loss.*

The largest group of these older widows and widowers (almost 50 percent) were not devastated by their spouses' deaths. They felt sad, missed their spouses, and had periods of intense longing for them, but they maintained relatively normal functioning and did not experience a delayed grief reaction when followed for four years. These individuals were described as resilient. There was no relationship between the quality of the prior marital relationship and resilience; that is, resilient people had satisfying as well as unsatisfying marriages, and knowing the quality of the prior relationship alone did not predict who would be resilient. In addition, these resilient people had been evaluated prior to the deaths of their spouses and were not found to be substantially different from others in the study— "they were not seen as cold and unsympathetic… nor were they exceptionally warm and sociable" (p. 70).

Though the characteristics of resilient people are not yet well known, Bonanno outlines some factors. Thinking or talking about the deceased person was more likely to bring feelings of comfort, happiness, and peace to those considered resilient. The surviving spouses could find joy in the memories of experiences they shared with the deceased spouse, and a sense that, though the person was gone, the relationship was not totally gone. Bonanno also reported that other studies reveal additional factors that are related to resilient people: they have "better financial resources, more education, and fewer ongoing life stressors to worry about; they are also likely to be in better physical health and to have a broader network of friends and relatives on whom they can rely both for emotional support and for helping with the details and demands of daily life" (p. 76). Resilient people are optimistic, believing that things will get better, they are more flexible in adapting to changing circumstances, and feel they have some control over how things turn out in their lives.

For those who were not described as resilient in the CLOC group, 15 percent initially showed intense grief symptoms that gradually declined until they were largely absent by the eighteen-month follow-up. The remaining 30 percent of study participants fell into one or another of three groups in about equal numbers: those for whom grief had become chronic and was still actively present after four years; those who were depressed both before and after the death; and a group who were depressed before the death but improved after the loss.

Several individuals in our group, according to their own accounts, could be described as resilient. These are individuals who, after their spouses died, missed them and were sad but whose functioning remained quite robust even so. Bill told us he was surprised at how soon after Alexis' death he felt at peace and content about the good life they'd had together. Most of our group would be described as those who had intense grief symptoms for some time after the death, but whose grief diminished gradually over time. No one in our group was chronically grieving or apparently depressed at the time of the interview. Two people in our group would be described as improving in overall functioning after the deaths of troubled spouses.

Supports for Grieving

Immediately after Brent's accidental death, my friends, sons, and brother took turns staying with me. My brother went with me to get Brent's ashes and managed the memorial service.

—Rachel

Friends were mentioned most often as a source of help for grieving spouses. Friends came to stay with the grieving, helped with funeral arrangements, listened, arranged outings and social times, and kept in contact beyond the initial time of loss. We also found, however, that friends were sometimes not helpful. After her husband's traumatic death, Maria told us:

I found that a few people in my life I thought I could count on could not tolerate my pain and abandoned me. Others were just a burden for me to be around, because they pitied me. I developed antennae for who was right for me to spend time with.

Patrick reported something similar:

I could not predict who would be helpful or not. I wanted to have contact with people who had also loved Elaine, yet I felt rejected and misunderstood by some of her friends. They turned down my invitations to have a meal together to ease my loneliness.

On the other hand, some friends and neighbors who weren't expected to be helpful, indeed were. So the newly widowed were both disappointed and pleasantly surprised by those who gathered around them. People relied on friends to help them during their grieving while also recognizing that they did not want to burden their friends. Relying on friends was more typical for widows than widowers. Family members were also a significant source of support, and, as with friends, family members sometimes were unable to be helpful to the grieving widow or widower.

Almost half the widows and widowers either sought psychotherapy or a grief recovery group to support their grieving process, and reported these contacts and relationships had been very helpful to them. Two of our widows started their own grief support groups. About one third of the group found activities, including return to work, in which they could focus their energies and have a sense of purpose. Other individuals reported benefiting from religious belief, meditation, sound healing, participation in rituals, reading, writing, or journaling. Two widows found writing to their deceased spouses each day comforting. Carol, a young widow, rented humorous movies so she could laugh. One widow started a memorial fund to help people with serious illnesses. In that way, some of her spouse's hardships were transformed into a benefit for others. Peggy performed acts of kindness in Stan's name to honor him.

A few individuals found themselves sleeping, drinking, or eating too much, and needing to develop healthier patterns. Learning how to be alone comfortably was important to several people. Maria told us that it was a challenge to wait patiently for what time can do in the healing process.

Deciding to date or cultivate a new friendship that evolved into a new love not only created possibilities but also facilitated grieving. Sandra spoke for these people when she said:

"Opening my heart helped to heal the brokenness."

The widowed reported how helpful it was when a new love encouraged or was comfortable with talk about the deceased person. Cornelia and Doug, who had each been widowed, noted that they appreciated not having to "dance around" how happy they had been in their previous relationships. In addition, a new love who understood something about the process of grieving and had the capacity to tolerate or even encourage the emotional expressions of grieving, helped to build trust and intimacy in a developing relationship. Certainly couples who have been able early on to talk about very difficult subjects, such as the death of a partner, feelings of overwhelming loss, confusion, and perhaps regrets, have laid a strong foundation for the future.

Overall, the people we interviewed seemed to have learned to live with the loss of a partner and allowed themselves to grieve in the many ways they were inclined, seeking what they found would support that process for them. Most employed multiple strategies. They had, or discovered, confidence that they would have meaningful lives again. This was a powerful force—to come to believe this great loss would forever mark their lives but not define their lives. It was obvious that there was neither a single way nor a right way to navigate this journey.

Chapter 4:

Taking the Leap

American scholar Joseph Campbell said:

We must be willing to get rid of the life we've planned so as to have the life that is waiting for us.

Though everyone's life takes unexpected turns, those who have experienced the death of a spouse can attest vividly to the validity of Campbell's wisdom. After one's spouse dies comes the awareness that life will never be the same and will not be what it has been; that things one has "always" done will no longer be done just that way. Every aspect of life can be altered, from the most mundane, such as the food one buys and prepares, to the most consequential, such as where one will live and how one will manage finances. What direction will life take now that the former direction has been dramatically altered? In this process of defining one's life anew, the possibility of dating or not, of having another partner or not, of marrying again or not, is significant.

Dating

Sandra, whose prior marriage to Alden had been good, described her own process clearly:

I looked inside, deep in my core with honesty.
I asked, "Who am I now that I'm not the 'we'?
What am I going to do, what choices am I going
to make as I remake myself?"

As she reconstructed her life, Sandra discovered that she wanted eventually to have another loving partner. Dating would have to be the first step.

Our widowed friend, Robert, told us that for him the process of considering dating began with the shift of his self-concept from being part of a "we" to being an "I," from being a married man to being a single man. He was aware of noticing whether a woman was available or not, and of thinking of single women he'd known before in a new way. He thought about whether a particular available woman was one he might like to know better or might pursue romantically.

In interviews of older widowers, social science researcher Deborah K. van den Hoonaard found that men spontaneously talked about the importance of having female relationships, not necessarily marriage, even before being asked about this topic. Van den Hoonaard interpreted the significance widowers placed on these relationships as:

"... an intrinsic part of being widowers. Their
ideas conformed to notions of masculinity that
define being a real man as always being inter-
ested in or involved with a woman" (a, p. 104).

In contrast, a small minority of the senior widows van den Hoonaard interviewed expressed an interest in having relationships with men. She found, however, as did we, that both widows and widowers express a wide variety of ideas and feelings about new loving partnerships.

While exploring the quality of the prior relationships of our widowed, we learned that the nature of those relationships alone did not determine whether or not an individual eventually had a new loving relationship. People who'd had very positive earlier relationships, as well as people who'd had very troubled earlier relationships, and those in between, were interested in new relationships. Intuitively, we might think that if a person had experienced a close, loving relationship with a partner who died, he or she would in time want to seek another. However, there are also reasons not to do so: believing that another relationship could never measure up to the previous one; enjoying independence; and avoiding new complicated familial entanglements. Similarly, having had a troubled relationship might dissuade a person from considering another potentially troubling one. On the other hand, a person might believe that one set of difficulties does not predict future problems in another relationship and welcome the chance for a fresh beginning.

A discussion about the possibility of having another loving relationship with one's partner prior to death could provide some direction and also relieve feelings of betrayal when some form of consent was given. Eight people in our group reported having discussed seeking a new partner with their spouses prior to death. All of these ailing spouses had indicated they wanted their partners to have other loving relationships. Peggy's husband, who died of cancer, told her he wanted her to move on, to be happy and share love again. What a gift that was. No one indicated that a spouse said he or she should not have other loving relationships, but two ailing women did advise their husbands about what kind of women to avoid after they died—too skinny, too young, and too needy.

Psychology professor Alinde Moore and social worker Dorothy Stratton wrote about their study of older widowers in their book *Resilient Widowers: Older Men Speak for Themselves.* They found that prior to their spouses dying almost one third of the fifty-one wives gave some kind of permission or prediction for their husbands to seek other intimate relationships or to marry after they themselves died. Interestingly, two of these men vowed not to remarry in order to prove the deceased wife's prediction wrong. In interviews with older widows, van den Hoonaard found that only a small number of widows had discussed the possibility of future relationships with their ailing husbands prior to their deaths.

More widowers than widows in our group had this discussion with ailing spouses, though the numbers in both groups were small. Could there be a trend for women to be more concerned about what would become of their husbands after the women die than men concerned about what would happen to their wives? If so, it would signal a cultural shift. Historically, women have been characterized as being so dependent on men, particularly financially, that their welfare would be in jeopardy should they be without a husband-provider. Over time, however, as women have become more financially independent, there is an awareness of how emotionally and socially dependent men are on women and the accompanying jeopardy to their welfare without a wife-companion.

Intention

> *I had no thoughts about future romance after Alexis died. My plan was to continue the major remodeling of our house and be on my own.*
>
> —Bill

Though consideration of another loving relationship would seem integral to the process of redefining oneself at some time after loss, six of our widows or widowers said they had not thought about it. All but one of them described their marriages very positively. The time between the deaths and meeting their new partners-to-be had been from a few months to two years.

For example, after Doug's wife died suddenly:

> *I enjoyed some traveling and had decided I could live alone quite comfortably. However, in the course of communicating for mutual support with a female friend whose partner had also recently died, I was surprised to find that I was beginning to have loving feelings for her. That ended my satisfaction with living alone.*

A couple of women who had been widowed when quite young expected to remarry and wanted to. Carol was in her mid-thirties when Peter died unexpectedly. Though Carol knew she wanted to marry again, she was not actively seeking a partner. She casually dated some men whom she concluded were unsuitable for marriage. She made a list of qualities she would like in a husband, as Peter's volatility had been a negative aspect in their marriage that she wanted to avoid. Still, she felt she was only tenuously out there in the dating world when her new love came along.

Several other people indicated that even though they were amenable to seeing others, they were not doing so with a serious relationship in mind. Ann's husband had died a year prior to her meeting Brad on the Internet.

> I was dabbling in the possibility of dating someone, and the Internet gave me many options about the pace at which I could go. That kind of freedom created less stress about venturing into dating territory, as I felt I had more control over the situation.

Trina's husband had been deceased for five years when she agreed to date Mike, whom she had met years earlier but still didn't consider the possibility for a serious relationship. In fact, like six of the other participants, Trina didn't think she would ever remarry. Ella, Trina, and Eleanor all said they would not marry again because of the pain they'd experienced with their spouses' deaths. They wanted to avoid being vulnerable to such pain again. Nonetheless, Ella is now engaged. Trina realizes, after being with Mike for seven years without marrying, that she is not protected from pain should he die.

Eleanor is not married, and at the time of the interview did not anticipate marrying Brandon, though she was very satisfied with their relationship of five years. She gave several reasons for her decision:

The pain of my first husband's death was so devastating I would not want to repeat that experience. I have reservations about having to be a caretaker if Brandon were to become ill. Also, there are substantial financial disparities and accompanying complications between us that are lessened by not being married.

Brandon and Eleanor were the one couple who had chosen to "live apart together," a type of relationship in which couples have an intimate relationship but do not share a common home.

John's relationship with Louise had been so filled with turmoil that John had no intention of marrying again, but after meeting Hannah and being surprised by the ease of their relationship, he changed his mind and they married. Cynthia's marriage had also been very difficult, and she rejected the idea of marriage because she was relishing her independence. However, except for the marriage certificate, her relationship with Scott certainly resembles marriage. It is very positive and solid. Again, with the people who talked with us, we found no direct correlation between the quality or length of the prior relationship and the intention or interest to remarry.

Van den Hoonaard's widowers also expressed ambivalence about marrying again. Though they spoke about deep loneliness after their wives had died, there were reasons not to remarry: relinquishing independence; betraying the deceased wife; possibly inheriting new health problems in a spouse; re-experiencing the pain of spousal loss—all serious considerations when contemplating new relationships. With the exception of relinquishing independence, these factors are heavily influenced by the prior loss through death.

More than half the people we interviewed were looking for a relationship, though not necessarily with the intention of marrying. Sandra had dated a man casually, but felt she was "walking in a desert knowing someone was waiting for her." Peggy described her intention as she continued dating:

After grieving heavily, I realized I was "rattling around" my house—adrift. I wasn't looking for another big love like the one I'd had with Stan, but for companionship.

The desire for companionship was echoed by many and was closely related to feelings of loneliness—a powerful motivator. Patrick was very lonely after his wife of fifty-seven years died:

Although in my eighties, I thought I might marry again. That's what my wife predicted. I didn't have much of a life of my own. Some I'd turned to for support and company had rejected me, and I didn't want to be a burden to my adult children. It was the loneliness that led me to seek out social contact through an exercise group. That's where I met my new wife.

It was the same for Cornelia:

I was stunned by how lonely I was a year after my partner died.

A well-known widow, Dolly Levi, from Thornton Wilder's play *The Matchmaker,* on which the musical *Hello Dolly*, by Jerry Herman and Michael Stewart is based, tells about her experience after her husband, Ephraim, died. Dolly was financially strapped and withdrew into herself.

> *"Yes, in the evenings, I'd put out the cat, and I'd lock the door, and I'd make myself a little rum toddy; and before I went to bed I'd say a little prayer, thanking God that I was independent—that no one else's life was mixed up with mine."*

So, this was her period of contentment. In time, however, Dolly realizes that, like a "colorless pressed leaf," she has become drab, without 'tear' or 'hope' that something or other would turn out well." With this awareness she vows to "rejoin the human race." Part of that rejoining becomes her intention to marry the wealthy but miserly Mr. Vandergelder so that she can spread his money around to do the good she thinks money should. While her intentions for marriage are less than entirely honorable, Dolly asks Ephraim for his "permission" to remarry, and in the musical sings the wonderful song *Before the Parade Passes By*, proclaiming her intention to be a part of life again before it's too late.

This wish to be a part of the kind of life that one imagines and a desire to have the pleasures of a loving relationship spurred some individuals in our group to actively seek a new partner. Peggy was motivated by wanting to share love again. Helen, whose partner had become abusive, felt "ready to be loved" again, as she had in the beginning of that earlier relationship. Eleanor, recounting how expansive love can be, wanted to share experiences with someone close to her. Similarly, Cornelia, who was sixty-five years old when her partner died, described thinking:

> *This can't be IT for me, my life winding up without a loving relationship. I want that kind of intimacy again.*

Brad, who had a young son when Becky died, chose to wait five years before entertaining the possibility of a new relationship. By then he felt it was important for his now adolescent son to see a loving adult relationship at home. That led him to an online dating service. Maria and Laura, each of whom also had young children when a spouse died, had waited more than two years before considering dating, aware that bringing a new person into her own life, also meant bringing a new person into the lives of their young children and must be done with care.

This group of active seekers had grieved the loss of partners but did not want to lose having intimate partnerships forever.

Meeting a New Love

> *I didn't want another relationship after Craig died, but my friends kept saying I was missing out on a big part of life.*
>   —Cynthia

It was not unusual for friends to urge widows and widowers to take a chance on loving again. Just as friends played a major role in supporting the bereaved, they again played a major role, sometimes as matchmakers. About one third of our group came together because mutual friends either urged a meeting, thinking there might be a fit between two people, or provided a venue for the individuals to meet. Persistence was often needed to encourage or persuade a widowed friend to try meeting someone, to enter that now foreign world.

Friends encouraged three of our couples to get together because each had been widowed, and friends believed they could support one another. Other people got together because they had known each other before as neighbors or coworkers or socially; were involved in activities where they met such as hiking, dancing, and exercising; or became acquainted on Internet dating sites. A small number met through family members.

Timing and Sparks: Is This for Real?

When I met Kirk there was a deep connection very quickly. We had a sense of "home" about each other.
—Peggy

The length of time between a spouse's death and beginning a new partnership varied among our participants. For six people in our group it had been less than six months since the death when they began to spend time with a person who later became a partner. Five of these individuals were men. In another group of six for whom it had been from one to three years since the death, the gender ratio was reversed, including only one man. About equal numbers of men and women had been widowed for over three years when they first spent time with their new loves.

Of course, these people were not new loves right away. How can one pinpoint a specific moment when a friend or companion becomes more? About half of the widows or widowers had dated others before meeting their new loves. Although most of these earlier dates had been casual relationships, a few relationships had lasted more than three years; but for half of all the widowed, once they met the new person, the relationship developed very quickly. Sandra and Paul were such a couple. Sandra had dated several men, one for quite a while, in the four years since Alden had died. She told us:

I hadn't felt drawn to commit to anyone until Paul, whom I'd known socially. Once we started seeing each other, I felt comfortable immediately. I felt no ambivalence about being with him; it felt special from the beginning—harmonious, respectful, open, and easy. We had no preconceived notions of where we were going; we were just enjoying the moments.

Carol's relationship with Andrew also went smoothly.

I felt attracted to him; he checked out on the list of qualities I desired in a potential spouse. I realized early in our time together that this relationship could be forever.

Tony, whose wife had died six months earlier, was surprised at the strength of his attraction to Jody; he pursued her right away, even though he still felt very sad about Linda's death. Cynthia had dated several men since her husband died; she enjoyed male companionship, but vowed never to have a serious relationship or remarry because she valued her independence.

That was before I met Scott. I started having fun in a way I hadn't experienced in a very long time. We could talk for hours. Within months I knew this relationship was different, and I wanted-ed to be with him always.

Rachel embarked on a deep introspective journey after Brent's sudden death. In time she realized she wanted to consider being with a woman. Even though this represented a major change, it felt right to her.

I dated a little and then met Mira through a mutual friend who thought we might be compatible. I was just looking for a fling until after we'd spent several intense days together. I was more attracted to her than I'd expected to be, and it was both exciting and disturbing. Our relationship grew steadily afterward.

After Penny's death, Cornelia decided to date men, though feeling guilty that she wanted another loving relationship and questioning whether she was betraying her love for Penny. Some women in her lesbian community felt betrayed by her, yet, like Rachel who changed her gender preference in a partner, Cornelia came to be confident with her decision.

Doug and I had known each other casually before, and we began talking more as we had each lost our partner and found emotional support from one another. Doug was the first to declare that he was having loving feelings toward me.

In time, I allowed myself to let in the possibility that I could care for him. I was drawn to him because he was introspective and self-aware, but it was also scary to think I could be in a real, loving relationship again.

The challenge for Alan in our growing relationship was his expectation that our love would feel the same as the love he'd had for Susan. It was not the same. I was grateful, though not happy, that Alan was honest with me about doubting his feelings for me were love. Once he realized that his loving me would not feel the same as his loving Susan, his heart was open to genuinely love again. With the barrier of comparison lifted, our relationship could thrive.

Ann had a similar experience when she and Brad first started dating. Not only were her feelings for Brad different than she'd had for Collin but the whole nature of the relationship was different. Though disconcerting initially, when she recognized that it would not be the same as before, Ann was delighted by the unique quality of this new relationship.

In this age of social media, online dating services played a role, even with some of our older couples. Match.com brought Peggy and Kirk together.

He was the first person I'd contacted. I felt an immediate, deep connection with him. We had similar values, interests, and lifestyles. This sense of connectedness fueled our growing devotion to each other.

Another Internet dating site, Greensingles.com, brought Ella and Hank together. As we learned earlier, Internet dating lent Ella a feeling of safety as she stepped into these relationship waters.

> *The relationship with Hank moved pretty fast, primarily through phone calls and emails because we lived in different parts of the country. I was attracted to his honesty, interests, spirituality, and humor. I felt surprised that neither the Internet nor our geographic distance prevented me from having strong feelings for him quickly.*

Even for couples whose relationships developed somewhat more slowly over time, there seemed to be a juncture where the line was crossed—where the people realized that this person, this relationship, was special and then invested seriously in it emotionally. For example, Sally had known Tom and Christine for many years before Christine died. Sally told us how her relationship with Tom began:

> *Sometime after Christine's death, I reached out to Tom and we began spending time together as friends, enjoying walking and talking. Later I learned that he didn't think I'd be attracted to him—he was older and thought he wasn't attractive enough for me, so he was surprised when I told him about my loving feelings for him and soon declared his for me.*

So it was for Laura and Brian after Jay's death:

> *Mutual friends had introduced us, but it was many months before we started to spend time together. The chemistry between us was great from the start. We had many common interests and*

shared activities, and because he was closer in age to me than Jay had been, in some ways I felt I'd gotten my life back. We proceeded slowly because I had a young child and wanted to gradually introduce Brian into my child's life.

Ann and Brad didn't have immediate chemistry:

After meeting online we saw each other casually, largely because we had both been widowed and shared that experience. Within months, however, our attraction to each other took off, and we were seeing each other every day. We also had younger children to consider, and moved at a pace we felt was respectful of them and of the parents who had died.

—Ann

Whether it had been a very short time or several years since a spouse's death, when something clicked between people, the pursuit of love ensued. There were impediments to this pursuit, for certain, but the pull toward companionship, love, intimacy, and a long-lasting relationship was strong.

Grieving and Loving

Loss, grief, and love can all exist together.

—Cornelia

When it came to moving into new loving relationships, the widows and widowers who shared their stories with us taught us a lot about the simultaneous process of grieving and finding new loves. What we had experienced in our own relationship was echoed by many; that is, for many, grieving the death of a spouse is not like suffering and healing from strep throat. One doesn't have the problem, take the treatment, and emerge free of the sore throat and ready to move on as though the illness had never existed. Grieving has neither a predictable and discrete course nor a predictable and discrete end for any individual, and grieving does not preclude falling in love. Many of the bereaved told us that while they were no longer in acute grief when they met their new loves, their grieving was not over. Those individuals who told us that they were intentionally looking for some kind of relationship reflected a readiness to move on.

It had been four years since Alden died when Sandra and Paul started to spend time together. Sandra felt her active grieving was over, but at times she was still emotional about her loss. Carol felt the same about her grief and spending time with Andrew, but he noticed she still talked about Peter a lot without realizing it. Lorraine told us:

> *I was still sleeping too much and feeling depressed following Christopher's death when I happened to meet Patrick. In our new relationship I found the solace I'd been searching for, and we helped each other grieve the relatively recent losses of our spouses.*

Helen and Nancy got together not long after Lisa died, and Helen felt she continued to grieve actively for another two years while also being in a loving relationship with Nancy. Like others, Helen was building a new relationship at the same time she was grieving the former one.

One of the first in-depth conversations Alan and

I had concerned how difficult life was for him without Susan, who had died nearly a year earlier. Emotional talks about Alan's experience of her illness and death, and his missing her profoundly, continued even as we began to know and eventually love one another. These conversations were an important part of the growing intimacy and trust between us. Grieving and loving were intermingled.

Some individuals felt their grieving was over when they met their new loves. Of this group, the majority had experienced the death two or more years earlier. Peggy's husband, Stan, had died one and a half years earlier:

> *I felt integrated about my love for Stan. I loved him without the pain of earlier grief, and was ready to claim life again.*

Carol described her experience this way:

> *I had felt grief in waves, sparked by a smell, a song, an item of clothing, but at the time Andrew came along, I felt healed and ready for a new relationship.*

Completed mourning was echoed by Rachel, who felt that grieving for her spouse and moving on to a new relationship were two distinct processes. She and Mira met more than three years after Brent's death, and Rachel felt her grieving was over.

Some people told us they felt their grieving would never be over. Maria explained her experience:

> *Grant died when we were in our thirties, and my grieving intensified again after my new husband*

and I separated many years later. The pain of the separation renewed my longing for Grant and the deep and loving relationship that had been taken from me with his tragic death.

When the promise of the new relationship was not fulfilled for Maria, the strong loving feelings for her first husband resurfaced. She longed for him and the hopes for a life they had planned.

Eleanor also described her grief as coming in waves and feels at some level she is still grieving Bruce's death ten years later. Yet she is very happy in her relationship with Brandon. For her, anniversaries, a movie or other event can trigger tender and sad feelings. Speaking of Bruce she said:

In some way I'm living for both of us; but even in grief, I don't stop living or loving.

Tony told us about grieving and loving simultaneously:

It was a blessing to be able to pursue life and love after Linda's death, and not withdraw into a shell. Yet my grieving goes on, and I think it may never go away completely but will coexist with my love for Jody. I still cry sometimes about Linda, even though I love Jody.

So memories of deceased spouses can still evoke feelings of great sadness and longing, but no one in our group had been crippled by these feelings or consumed by them. The feelings came now and then, but most of the time lives were lived fully in the present, in the context of new loving relationships. How refreshing it was to learn that grieving and falling in love could be interwoven tracks in one's life after the death of a spouse. Eleanor told us:

> *Grieving over a spouse with whom you've had a good relationship doesn't negate having the desire for a new relationship and love.*

These couples exemplified what the research found that Bonanno writes about. The belief that the loss of a spouse predestines one to a long period of deep anguish from which there is no recovery is a myth. Further, the belief that a certain period of time, say, the commonly touted magical one year, should elapse before making any changes is also a myth. These myths have powerful effects on the bereaved and on their friends and family members, as we will see in the next three chapters.

Chapter 5

Challenges

Challenges, roadblocks, problems, bumps in the road—whatever you call them, not all was smooth sailing for these new couples. Some of these challenges prompted us to undertake the project that led to this book. Of course, challenges to new relationships are nothing new, but the nature of many of these challenges was difficult because the new coupling occurred in the shadow of a death. In this chapter we will consider some of the challenges to new relationships after a death: differences from challenges after divorce; the presence of the deceased; and geographic distance. Because issues with children were of particular importance to our couples, we will consider these separately in chapter 6. Chapter 7 will consider issues about timing of new relationships.

Different From After Divorce?

I had faced problems before in a new relationship after divorce. Those problems were quite different from those I encountered with Milton, whose wife had died.
—Margaret

How does finding a new relationship after the death of a spouse differ from finding a new relationship after divorce? There are some important factors that differentiate the two situations.

Some marriages end with mutual agreement of the parties. In most typical divorces, however, a person is either the one who decided to end the marriage or the one whose spouse decided to end the marriage. Either way, the people involved have had an unsatisfactory experience in the relationship, maybe even an unbearable or abusive one. It's not unusual, therefore, to have feelings of failure—failure to be successful in being married and all that marriage entails. People often feel they had poor judgment in choosing their partners in the first place, or didn't see, or chose to ignore, obvious potential problems and should have known better. The likely emotional roller coaster may have included questions about love, capacity for wrestling with problems and finding solutions, and anguish over changes that were unforeseen.

In addition to feelings of failure, divorced people are often sad, even the partner who decided to leave. Both partners lose the life they had envisioned with each other and all the hopes and dreams that were alive when they became partners. There may also be great sadness for the children of those partners, who will no longer have parents who live together.

Often, anger also plays a part in divorce. The people who leave may be angry that, in their eyes, their partners were unable to do or be what the relationship required in order to flourish. "If only he or she would have... then it would have worked." The people who are left may be angry that their partners abandoned the relationship, didn't try hard enough to sustain it, and took the easy way out. If one's partner had an affair or engaged in illegal or immoral behavior, a sense of betrayal may also color the emotional picture of the divorced person. It can be devastating to discover that a person you were closest to and trusted has stepped outside the marital contract.

For the person who desired to continue the marriage but whose partner left, rejection can be added to the list of strong feelings experienced during a divorce. Rejection can spark feelings of "not being good enough or not having enough" that undermine confidence in seeking new love relationships. Further, if there are children, assets, or business relationships that must be jointly attended to after the divorce, the continuing relationship may pose problems that persist into the future.

Thus the backdrop for a divorced person considering moving on to another relationship presents many challenges: an unsatisfactory experience in marriage; possible feelings of failure, anger, betrayal, and rejection; and the possibility of bringing along problems with the ex-spouse. This is a different constellation of factors from those experienced by the bereaved. While both divorced and widowed people experience sadness in the loss of their dreams and their lives are forever changed, in the case of divorce there is intent by at least one of the partners for the marriage to end. The vast majority of widows and widowers we interviewed had spouses who wanted their marriages to go on, and, as important, the deceased spouses were often beloved. Even in the event of suicide, the driving force of the act may have more to do with inner demons than with the intent to end a marriage. Also, while the spouse of a divorced person may be troublesome, he or she still exists in the flesh. The deceased spouse does not.

Therefore the emotional "package" with which the widowed approach a new relationship generally differs from that of the divorced. Both have joys and challenges, and there can even be similarities in individual cases, but some fundamental factors are different.

The Deceased's Shadow

One factor that was not a major problem for our group was feeling threatened by the "shadow" of the deceased person. Over half of the group of new partners spontaneously reported that they were not threatened by the attachment and love that had existed between the widowed and their deceased partners. In fact, for some new partners, the widow or widower's previous long and happy marriage was an asset. There was a belief that a person who had been in a long, satisfying relationship had qualities that were attractive and would bode well for a new relationship. Surely, people who have been happily married for many years are likely to be caring, loyal, persistent, able to meet hardships and able to solve problems. Not that the deceased partners were ignored—quite the contrary: most couples spoke easily of their former relationships, and there was rarely a feeling of being negatively judged or compared with the deceased person. These couples could talk about and describe earlier partners and experiences in a way that did not generate insecurity in their new partners.

Making negative comparisons to a previous relationship is a big red flag, a warning of troubled waters. Such comparisons can represent many different dynamics that if not resolved could erode a budding relationship. A widow or widower who negatively compares a new person to a deceased partner is not a good candidate for a new loving relationship. Any connection that requires someone to live up to another is on shaky ground. It may signal the widow or widower's continuing attachment to the previous relationship in a way that prevents the development of a new attachment, and suggests an emotional lack of readiness to move on. It may signal a desire to reshape someone in the likeness of the previous partner, which is a recipe for discord or disaster. A healthy relationship requires that each person be seen and appreciated for who he or she is individually—the good, the bad, the quirks, the whole person.

That the new partners of our widows and widowers did not feel threatened by the deceased's shadow seems as much a testament to the widows and widowers giving of themselves to their new loves as to the self esteem of their new partners. The fact that our group represented a somewhat older demographic may also play a part; that is, the majority of new partners had considerable life experience, successful careers and prior relationships, and felt secure about themselves as individuals. Several people mentioned that what they had learned in earlier relationships would serve them well in the new relationship. Other new partners expressed appreciation for the widow or widower not making unfavorable comparisons between them and deceased spouses. Paul was just one example. He moved into Sandra's house when they married and said Sandra led the way in making him feel comfortable by not idealizing her deceased husband.

The memories or reputations of the deceased did, however, present some insecurities. Sally told us her feelings about Tom's earlier long marriage:

Tom and Christine had been married for over forty years when Christine died. When Tom and I married, I felt intimidated by the length of time they had been together and all they had shared in their lives. I knew that at our more advanced ages we would not be as fortunate, but I am grateful to Christine—she helped shape Tom into the wonderful person he is.

Jody said:

Tony's deceased wife was "larger than life." I knew I couldn't compete with that legacy so decided I would be different in my own way.

Jody came to terms with the necessity of being an authentic person. Tony was accepting of her, but family and friends were judgmental. Becoming comfortable with herself helped Jody deal with the comparisons community members made between her and Tony's deceased wife.

Margaret shared those feelings:

I knew that Milton's first wife had been beloved and on a pedestal in the eyes of family members.

I couldn't compete with that ghost, and learned to be content with being who I am and not being on a pedestal. Had I been in my twenties or thirties I'm not sure I could have felt that confident about myself.

In another way, Nancy struggled with Lisa's shadow in her new relationship with Helen:

I didn't understand for a while why Helen was still sad. Lisa had been abusive to her during her illness, and I knew Helen felt some relief after Lisa's death because of that. I came to know that loss could be hard even if a relationship was bad.

I struggled initially with the fact that my happiness in being with Alan was possible only because another woman had died. Those feelings of sadness and a strange kind of guilt were compounded by the thought that Susan would not see her boys grow into men and perhaps have families, and she would not get to be a grandmother, a role that was precious to me. Cornelia, herself a widow and attracted to a widower, said similarly:

How can we open our hearts when we loved so deeply before? I will always be grieving. Is it all right to fall in love and feel this happy?

Thus close romantic relationships that develop in the aftermath of someone's death carry a unique characteristic: the reality that another person's life ended before the new relationship began. Further, the surviving partner may wrestle with whether it's okay to love again when his or her deceased spouse has been robbed of life and loving. This is akin to the survivor's guilt that soldiers recount when they live on after fellow soldiers die. Whether recognized consciously or not, these are ways in which the deceased partner or partners were an integral part of new relationships, but did not overshadow the new relationships to their detriment. The vast majority of our couples chose to acknowledge the deceased spouses openly rather than make a ghostly, hidden presence of them.

Our couples reported several other obstacles that were not necessarily different from any other couple forging a new life together:

- Learning about and accommodating the differences in upbringing from different cultural backgrounds, such as manners, favorite foods, music, holiday celebrations.
- Accepting a partner's pets.
- Adapting to different life rhythms such as sleeping and eating times.
- Getting used to having children or grandchildren around who were not your own, especially for those who had previously not had children at all.
- Trying to fit in with friends whose topics of interest or pastimes or "inside jokes and stories" were foreign.

Geographical Distance

Another factor that was initially considered an impediment, but not a deal breaker, was geographic distance. Living in different states or even countries can be a hurdle in any developing relationship, not only when spousal death is a factor. Thanks to phones, email and Skype, couples who were not close geographically found their frequent electronic contact meaningful, even though they would have preferred being together. Plane travel made being together possible. Alan and I lived in separate states for over a year before we were married and for two years after.

> *We worked out a schedule of visits, traveling to each other's homes every three weeks or so for a week. While for us that level of contact was acceptable, even exciting and new for a while, it perpetuated much of the loneliness we both wanted to escape. However, it allowed me a long time to wrestle with moving and leaving family, friends, and my practice. On the positive side, the accrued frequent-flyer miles served us well for years!*
>
> —Janice

Other couples, who were retired, found that alternating between their homes for weeks or even months at a time suited them well until they were able to be together in one place permanently. Peggy and Kirk, though in the same geographic area, alternated living in each of their houses for several months to decide which house would best suit them in the long term.

Many couples who were geographically distant at first relied on phone calls that were both frequent and often lengthy. Email was another way of linking that allowed the exchange of sensitive feelings and thoughts. Using Skype enhanced the personal quality of these long-distance interactions. Of the couples we talked with who had met "electronically," none were disappointed or dissuaded once they had face-to-face contact. We know, however, that it is possible that a person is not as appealing in person as he or she seems over the phone or through written words. Those who were disappointed and broke off a relationship after seeing one another were, for obvious reasons, not in our group of couples.

Chapter 6

Children's Reactions to New Loves

My daughter was very close to her father. She really missed him. It was hardest for her to see that my relationship with Patrick was becoming serious, and she was protective of me—she asked Patrick directly if he loved me.

—Lorraine

Of all the challenges encountered by new couples, those concerning children of the deceased parents were the most upsetting. Whether the children of departed parents were young or already adults, their resistance to new parental relationships presented significant emotional obstacles. Of course, people newly in love would like everyone else to share in their joy, especially their children, who are living reminders of the family that once was and are of special importance to the surviving parent. Naturally, not all parent-child relationships are positive even before the death of a spouse or before a new relationship is a reality. A parent's moving toward new love could increase the distance or friction with a child. It is interesting to note that none of the new partners who hadn't experienced the death of a spouse reported having children who objected to a relationship with a widow or widower.

Challenges with Young Children

In our group of parents, for those with young children whose parent had died, accepting a new person in the surviving parent's and therefore the child's life, was usually difficult, unless the child was too young to be aware of the loss. Walking the fine line between empathizing with the feelings of a young child and choosing to have a new loving partner is a major task for surviving parents. One such situation was that of Laura, whose daughter, Carrie, was seven years old when her father died.

> *Although Carrie liked Brian, she also resisted being close to him and resented that he was taking over time with me, whom she'd had to herself for several years. Every new development the relationship brought was a challenge: the engagement, marriage, moving to another house. Carrie created an altar for her father that helped comfort her.*

Brian's and Laura's awareness of and support for Carrie's altar sent a strong message that they valued and respected Carrie's feelings of longing for her father. In addition, they communicated the fact that they valued and respected Jay as Carrie's father and that Brian was not going to take Jay's place. Over the next several years, Laura and Brian spent hours talking about how to proceed in a way that both allowed their own relationship to grow and also eased Carrie's worries and resentment about Brian. Their patience and concern really paid off. Now, ten years later, Carrie said, "Our family is awesome."

When Barbara married Larry just over a year after his wife had died, his two daughters were very young—three and five years old. It seemed that everyone felt sorry for these little girls who didn't have a mother. Barbara thought they had been indulged in ways that were not healthy for them. She felt her first task as their "new mother" was to create structure for them and set appropriate limits. She took her role very seriously and was not always appreciated by some family members, sometimes not even by Larry who was more permissive that she. It was difficult for Barbara, who took over the major parenting role, to see the girls run to their daddy when hurt, or go to dad when older because he rarely denied them anything.

In order to help the girls with their grieving, they participated in a support program for children who had experienced major losses. Barbara and Larry also kept photos of the girls' biological mother prominently displayed in their home, and Barbara especially made an effort to talk about their biological mother, for example, reminding them how proud she would have been about their accomplishments. In these ways, Barbara acknowledged that the girls' biological mother was an important figure in their lives in spite of how young they were when she died. Raisng another woman's children was challenging.

Brad had two young children when he and Ann became seriously involved five years after Brad's first wife died. Although Brad's daughter was accepting of Ann, his son resented that Brad could have another wife but he, the son, couldn't have another mother. It was not Ann specifically that was the obstacle, but the idea of Brad having a new partner.

This astute observation is very difficult for children and parents alike. Also, it is true: a child cannot have another biological mother or father, but adults can have many loving relationships if they choose. When a child is sad and missing the deceased parent, the surviving parent's attempts to reassure the child that everything will be all right are doomed to failure, as will be any attempt to present the new partner as a substitute mother or father. These approaches are simply placebos and deny the reality of the child's feelings. The parent must acknowledge the child's sadness and longing repeatedly so that the child feels heard and understood, not alone and abandoned. It would have been unwise for Brad to try to persuade his son with words that Ann could be a surrogate mother for him.

Ann also had a son who struggled with this new relationship, feeling that his mother was being disloyal to his deceased father. The son expressed his resentment through rude behavior and sarcasm until Ann learned that betrayal was the core issue. They then had a talk about his feelings and the nature of love.

I explained that my love for Brad didn't diminish the love I'd had for his dad. This awareness helped him change his attitude and behavior. He apologized to Brad and me for having been rude, and began to accept the fact that Brad would be a part of his life too.

Such situations pose a basic question: can a child understand that a parent is in love with someone new yet still loves and values the child's deceased parent? Adults also struggle with this issue, particularly if they've not had the experience personally. Ann's son was old enough to hear and understand that his mom still loved his father and that her love for Brad was different and separate. One similarity that children can understand about love is that parents love their first child and their second child and as many as come along. Each one is loved. Children experience this in another way as well: they love their parents, siblings, grandparents, aunts, uncles, cousins, friends, and pets. Love is not finite; rather, there is an infinite amount. Coming to understand this can free children to accept parents in new loving relationships as well as care for, even love, the new partners themselves.

Challenges with Adult Children

Most of the couples in our group had older children, not younger ones. Nearly half the couples we interviewed had experienced problems with adult children in the course of their coming together; some had been resolved, others had not. One of John's grown sons had been rude to Hannah, and John was still waiting for an apology. In the meantime, the relationship between father and son had become distant. Others experienced less overt reactions, but noted that phone calls or emails were not promptly returned or that responses were not as warm and loving as in times past. Both Joe and Patrick faced challenges not with their own children but with a child's spouse who had been particularly close to the now deceased mother-in-law. Patrick told us his son-in-law:

...had difficulty seeing me with another woman. He'd had a special fondness for Elaine and declared he would not be calling my new wife "Mother" as he had Elaine.

Two of George's three sons also disliked seeing him in a serious relationship with another woman, even though Lily had been dead for more than two years. They left George and Marianne's wedding party early and have chosen not to attend large family gatherings that include Marianne's grown children.

My experience with Alan's two sons was similar. It was difficult for them to see him in a relationship with another woman.

They were distant, and isolated themselves from my family and friends when there were opportunities to be together, including our wedding party. Alan often had to choose whether to be with his sons or with the rest of the group.

Seeing Alan caught between his sons and me was particularly painful. I wanted his boys to be a part of our new relationship and to offer them some comfort for the loss of their mother. I am prone to be active in attempts to eliminate discomfort if possible. Alan is more prone to let things be, even if he's uncomfortable. Alan was waiting for this tension with his sons to resolve on its own. I was trying to resolve it through letters to the boys, whom I saw only infrequently. They were essentially strangers to me and I to them. Neither of these approaches—Alan's waiting it out or my trying to establish a relationship and understanding through letters—was successful. We did not learn from them what was troubling them, and therefore could not attempt a solution.

Gradually, over many years, Alan's sons came to accept the fact that their dad and I would be together. One of them even decided to call me "Mom." Of course, it was never my intention, or even a possibility, to replace their mother, but I'm happy to be a second mom. Still, years of personal distance and awkwardness might have been avoided.

Milton's two sons were among the adult children who spoke with us. One of his sons, Eric, provided considerable insight into his difficulties with Milton's new relationship with Margaret. Eric had been affected by Milton's deep sadness when June died, but had little contact with his dad for a time because of issues in his own life. When a holiday brought them all together, Eric couldn't reconcile the bereaved dad he'd seen almost a year before with the new happy dad—it seemed too big an emotional leap in too short a time. Eric later reflected on this period when he changed his attitude:

> *I saw that my behavior was causing my dad pain. I really examined my feelings and realized that because I loved my dad, I could be happy for his happiness. As it turns out, Margaret is a great person.*

Milton's other son took time to warm up to the idea of his dad having a new love. Part of his struggle was with this new woman taking his father's, and therefore his own, last name when they were married. That made Margaret a part of the family group in a way that was difficult for him to embrace. Only by asking him directly was Milton able to discover what it was that was bothering him. He never would have guessed it was related to the family name.

Tony's adult children were worried about their deceased mother's belongings:

> *Understandably, when Jody moved into the house that had been Linda's and mine, my children were concerned about what would happen with their mother's things. Many objects that meant a lot to them—clothing, jewelry, china— I gave to my children and their spouses. When Jody and I combined our households, we labeled our furniture and artwork so our children, on both sides, would know which family would receive each of these pieces.*

It's easy to imagine how difficult it is to see another woman in "Mother's kitchen," using her utensils, dishes, cups and glasses, sitting in the furniture your mother chose, or setting your mother's table. Likewise, seeing another man in "Father's garage or shop," using his tools and sitting at his place at the table or in his favorite chair is equally hard. Similarly, for children of a deceased parent it can be jolting simply to see the surviving parent enjoy the company of a new potential partner. These situations are stark reminders that the other parent is gone—gone forever—and there's nothing like a new relationship to confront others with the finality of the loss. It is not easy for a child of any age to understand that the surviving parent's moving on to another relationship does not mean that the deceased parent is forgotten or that the prior relationship is not still cherished. Further, family members who are still actively grieving can be perplexed and troubled by a widow or widower who appears to be enjoying life again. This bears repeating: it can be troubling and even seem like a betrayal to still-grieving family members when a widow or widower appears to be enjoying life again.

Doug's daughter and granddaughter expressed this clearly by echoing what Brad's younger son said:

> *You can have another love, but I can't have another mom and I can't have another grandmother.*

A conflict in values created tension between Trina and her adult daughter. Though her daughter liked Mike, she was unhappy that Trina and Mike were living together without marrying. Trina felt strongly about not remarrying because of the pain she'd experienced with her first husband's death. When her daughter more fully understood her mother's feelings and desire to protect herself, she could accept Trina's decision.

Researchers Moore and Stratton, and van den Hoonaard, who interviewed older widowers and widows, found tension with adult children consistent with that in our group. These children felt that their fathers' desire for another wife was a betrayal of their deceased mothers, or that their fathers or mothers were seeking new relationships too soon after their spouses' deaths. Moore and Stratton speculated what some of our group told us: that children are hurt that a widower can have another wife and replace that missing role in their lives, but the children can't have another mother. Two of the widowers interviewed by van den Hoonaard had chosen to be in relationships with women over the strong objections of their children. These men's relationships with their children were seriously compromised; nonetheless, their allegiance was to their independence and choices and to these new relationships.

There is a conundrum for a child whose parent has died, particularly if the parent was beloved. A child loses not only the deceased parent but also the mother-father couple—"my parents." The child grieves both, just as the surviving parent grieves the loss of the partner and the partnership. If the surviving parent becomes interested in a new relationship before the child has grieved and accepted the parental loss, it can seem too soon. This may be true even though the child likely wishes for his or her parent not to be alone or unhappy. The child can therefore be caught between negative feelings about a new parental love relationship and wanting the parent to be happy (more about timing in chapter 7).

In our group, it was twice as likely for sons to have difficulty with a parent becoming involved in a new loving relationship than for daughters, particularly when it was a mother who had died. Why is this so? It might be that some boys and men have special emotional dependence on their mothers, which increases their vulnerability to their mothers' dying. That could result in their resistance to fathers moving on when moving on is so difficult for the sons. It's also possible that because females in general are more relationship oriented than males, a daughter might find it more natural or acceptable for a parent to want to find a new close relationship after being widowed. Conversely, van den Hoonaard found that adult daughters whose widowed fathers have come to depend on them might resent a new romantic interest intruding on their space.

Children Welcoming New Loves

We also found the opposite: children welcoming and accepting new relationships. Some younger children and many adult children were happy about their parent having a new love. As would be expected, adult children particularly felt responsible for trying to help their grieving parents both practically and emotionally, and thus often seemed relieved that a new partner would take over these roles. In fact, a few children took quite an active role in encouraging a parent not only to expand his or her social life but also to look in earnest for a new partner. Some parents found it challenging to be gracious toward their children's urgings—balancing their own desire for independence with their children's concern for their well-being. Other adult children genuinely liked the new partner and were just delighted that their parent had rediscovered the joys of a loving relationship. Sharon felt her children were happy because she had gotten "out of their hair."

Sandra's daughter, Lori, told us about her feelings regarding her mother. After Lori's father died, Lori worried about Sandra, who lived in a big house in a relatively isolated place and had always been a very social person. Lori was glad when her mom first started dating, believing that Sandra was not meant to be alone. Initially, however, neither Lori nor her siblings liked the men their mother dated. They told her so and urged her to be cautious, but when Paul came along, they all were thrilled. In fact, Lori knew Paul casually and had thought he would be a good match for her mom. She told us after they were together:

> *I knew that Paul was a good mate for my mother because of the way he looked at her. And, he is the love of her life.*

Lori loves Paul too. He has always accepted Sandra's children and not been jealous of these close relationships. The presence of Paul in Sandra's life also relieved Lori of some emotional responsibility for her mom, which she especially appreciated when she was faced with some major demands in her own life. But most of all, it's knowing her mother is both loved so much and loves so much that brings Lori joy.

Trina's daughter, Karen, told us a somewhat similar story about her mother. When her father died, Karen was living in another state and knew her mother was very lonely. She thought her parents had enjoyed a good marriage and assumed that Trina would want to have that kind of close relationship again. Karen also knew that she could not fill the void. In hindsight, she suspects that she was probably too forceful in urging her mother to date, and knows that some early dates were not very positive. Once Trina began seeing Mike, however, her dating experience changed for the better and Karen was delighted for her mom. When Karen got to know Mike, she found he was a great guy.

> *I love him, too—how could I not? He loves my mother, loves me and my boys, and is better to all of us than my own father's parents. I believe that my mom wanting to be in a loving relationship again honors my deceased father, with whom I was very close.*

Chapter 7

Timing: is it Too Soon?

A friend told me that it would have been nice for someone new to come along in five years, but not now only two years after Beth's death.

—Doug

The timing of a new relationship was problematic for family and friends alike who thought that the bereaved person was moving on too soon after the death. This belief and the strong feelings it can generate are not new. In 1600, Shakespeare wrote of Hamlet's distress about his mother marrying his dead father's brother within a month of the king's death. Of course, his grief is compounded later by anger and pursuit of revenge when he learns that this same uncle murdered his father. We encountered no murders, but the timing of new relationships could evoke strong reactions.

Tony was only one of our group who had this experience with his children. He was surprised that he was drawn to Jody so soon after Linda's death, because he was still grieving her loss. Moving too quickly was also a problem for friends. Bill and Kate got together not long after Alexis's death, and some of Bill's friends disapproved. Both Bill and Tony fit the profile of resilient men in the face of loss according to Bonanno, as discussed in chapter 3. Each loved his wife deeply and grieved the loss but was not devastated and subsequently welcomed finding new love. Others in our group told us they were judged or abandoned by friends who thought they had become involved with new people too soon.

Several of Milton's relatives resisted accepting Margaret into his life. Margaret said:

> *They were emotionally distant, and I was uncomfortable around them. One relative accused me of isolating Milton because Milton now preferred spending time with me.*

It is likely that these "resisters" were still grieving and not ready to move on. A friend of ours, Robert, made an observation about the pace of his grieving compared with that of family members and friends of his deceased wife Gloria. When the one-year anniversary of her death approached, family members and friends called to offer their sympathy and support. They were very emotional, even more than Robert himself. Puzzled, Robert concluded that because he continued to occupy the house he and Gloria had shared, where he saw reminders of her daily, he had been actively grieving her every day for the past year—her absence was literally all around him. However, family members and friends living in other states were busy with their own lives and mostly recalled Gloria on special occasions such as holidays and the date of her death. Literally, Robert had more opportunity to adapt to life without her than they had.

Ella discovered:

I was surprised that I could love both Richard, who had died, and Hank, so deeply. It revealed something to me about our cultural myopia— that we can have only one big love. It is obviously not true.

Due to the great diversity of social and cultural influences in the United States today, there are no clear guidelines that dictate appropriate timing for considering or engaging in dating or marriage after a partner's death. Historically, in many cultures and religious traditions, there have been and continue to be rules, particularly for the behavior of widows. In her book *The Mourner's Dance,* journalist Katherine Ashenburg describes customs past and present that influence widows' and widowers' behavior as a part of mourning. Victorians practiced an extended period of mourning, as much as several years, requiring relative isolation from which one gradually reemerged into active life. As with some other cultures, women's clothing transitioned from black to lighter colors, signaling to others the bereaved's return to a fuller social life.

In the early 20th century in the United States, these customs began to shift. Marion Harland's *Complete Etiquette,* published in 1914, cautions about attitudes toward widows and widowers:

"Don't judge the behavior of the newly bereaved. The heart knoweth its own bitterness and if that bitterness can be sweetened by some genial outside influence, let others hesitate to condemn the owner of the heart from seeking

that sweetness. Those whom we have lost, if they were worth loving, would be glad to know that our lives were not all dark" (p. 140).

While there was a trend in the early 1900s that shortened the period of bereavement and the markers thereof, the transition was gradual. As Ashenburg reports, however, by the 1960s, etiquette books were recommending that the widow or widower quietly withdraw for a few months and then return to regular life, implying that not to do so was abnormal. This shift gave way ultimately to the broadly held idea that each person's timeline is unique to him or her and the situation, and that there are no strict guidelines that determine appropriate timing for dating or marrying after the death of a spouse.

Along with other religious and ethnic groups, however, Greek Orthodox and Orthodox Jewish customs still proscribe specific time periods for mourning. The Greek custom is to wear black clothing to signify one's vulnerability. Greek widows may extend their expected mourning period of one year to the rest of their lives. Jewish customs forbid remarriage during the first thirty days after a spouse's death but provide little specific guidance after that period. For the widowed who do not hold strong religious or cultural traditions, guidelines about mourning are not clear or are absent altogether. While "to each his own" gives the bereaved much freedom, we've found that it also brings problems.

There is an interesting paradox in all this: people who are grieving notice that others, even they themselves, are surprised or dismayed by how long grieving can go on—remnants of grieving can last for years. Grievers can feel rushed to get over the loss of their deceased loved ones and are mindful of not wanting to burden friends and family for too long with their mourning. Being around people who are sad, upset, and crying makes most of us uncomfortable, and we wish for them, and for us, that they will soon feel better—but not too soon, especially when it comes to the bereaved widow or widower pursuing a new close relationship. This is a delicate balance if one needs the approval of others. Our couples seemed content with their decisions, even though they were not without consequences. Sometimes these decisions compromised relationships with family members and friends.

This notion of timing is an intriguing one. Does anyone really know when an attraction—physical, emotional, spiritual—might occur? As we discussed in chapter 4, we believe it's not a given that when a person experiences the loss of a spouse, he or she must complete a period of grieving in order to be ready to have a new loving relationship, yet that is a common belief in our culture. Our bereaved individuals have taught us otherwise. Grieving and new loving can be interwoven, and, as we'll see in chapter 9, new loves can promote healthy grieving.

Chapter 8

Resolutions: Successful or Not

This chapter considers resolution of issues pertaining to finances and then resolution of issues with family and friends, learning from our couples' experiences.

Finances

All couples must deal with financial issues, some of which are common to couples who've gotten together later in life and to those who've gotten together after the death of a spouse, such as the people in our group. Older people are likely to own houses, cars, furniture, jewelry, artwork, pensions, retirement funds, and other assets. Even though we didn't specifically ask about how they were dealing with financial concerns, some couples told us spontaneously how they handled income, bills, and assets. They identified two primary issues: day-to-day living expenses and estates.

Deciding how to address day-to-day living expenses required communication and a plan, since paying for rent or mortgages, utilities, cars, food, clothing, and medical bills is essential and payment can't be postponed. We learned from our couples that there were a variety of ways to share these expenses. One couple volunteered that they put their income into one account for paying all of their expenses. Another couple maintained a joint account for shared expenses such as mortgage, car, food, and utilities. Each also had a separate account for personal expenses such as clothing, medical care, and travel. Milton and Margaret had such an arrangement. They had sold the houses in which they'd been living before they married, and purchased a new house together. They equally shared expenses for the new house, their cars, food, and joint travel. Each was separately responsible for the cost of individual activities, solo travel, and maintenance of real estate owned separately. A similar combination of joint and separate funds was the most common arrangement couples told us about. Only one couple, who also maintained separate houses, kept their incomes and expenses separate. For this couple, there was considerable disparity in income between the two individuals.

Whatever plan a couple adopted, the most important features were being able to discuss money, a difficult and often taboo subject, and satisfaction on the part of each individual with the agreed-upon arrangement. As in most things, we learned that there was no right or wrong way, and what worked for one couple might be unsuitable for another.

Protecting assets and estates for each individual in a new partnership, and for their respective children or heirs, becomes a critical consideration for people who bring such resources to their relationships. Children who have lost a parent have a vested interest in the surviving parent's preserving assets for them and for their own children. This poses a different dynamic from the remarriage of parents following divorce. In that case, both parents already have divided assets and are still available to their children. The parent who has died, however, has no voice (unless he or she has left a will), and the surviving parent therefore has sole control of the estate.

Consultation with an attorney and/or accountant is wise when making decisions about assets and estates, particularly as state laws differ throughout the United States. Chris Kenady, a Washington State attorney who has focused in part on estate planning, offered some suggestions. She cautioned strongly against leaving these important considerations to the best intentions and trust of others, even, or perhaps especially, family members. Trusting that others will fairly and judiciously share assets following death is risky. As we all know, inheritance issues can divide a family and often have strange and unexpected effects on people, particularly in times when emotions are running high. Clear directions can avert much conflict.

According to Kenady, trusts offer a useful strategy in these situations. Trusts can be configured in many different ways to accommodate the special requirements of the situation, and serve to protect each partner as well as any children or other heirs they may have. Upon one individual's death, a proportion of that individual's assets can be made available to the survivor until that person's death, when the remaining assets are distributed to heirs. In that way a surviving spouse has access to income without depleting the assets, thereby preserving them for heirs while not having his or her well-being jeopardized in the interim.

For example, Alan and I have trusts individualized for our wishes. Our house is owned jointly by our separate trusts. When one of us dies, the survivor may live in the house as long as he or she wishes or until death. The house then reverts to Alan's children and my children in proportional shares. This provision precludes the need for one of us to lose our home just after losing our life partner. It's easy to imagine how stressful it would be to sustain these two major losses at the same time.

Other steps people can take in estate planning, according to Ms. Kenady, include altering wills and/ or changing the beneficiaries of stock and investment funds or insurance policies. She also underscored what we found to be true in our group: ensuring that children are aware of the arrangements helped to ease tensions and assure heirs that their interests have been considered. This is true of family possessions as well as financial assets. How devastating it would be for children who had already lost a parent to also lose treasured belongings that reminded them of their parents.

Betty and Rex confronted financial issues with Betty's children even before they married. Betty's family has considerable financial assets. Though her children urged her to meet other men after their father died, when the relationship between Betty and Rex became serious, her children began to worry about the future of the assets, even though they liked Rex. A couple of Betty's children were "dispatched" to check out Rex, determine what his intentions were, and to advise their mother. Rex told us:

> *I understood her children's concerns and re-*
> *spected their being protective of their mother.*
> *I assured them of my honorable intentions and*
> *love for their mother, and told them that our as-*
> *sets would be separated, leaving their mother's*
> *estate intact.*

Rex's ability to see the situation from Betty's children's viewpoint was mature and wise. In the end, Betty's and Rex's children and grandchildren have blended very well and have become one big happy family. Dealing in a straightforward way with the often taboo subject of money cleared the emotional path for Betty and Rex and their respective families. If doubts, suspicion, and resentment had been allowed to fester, the outcome would have been very different.

Friends and Families

Friends who deserted the people we talked with, either when they were grieving or when they were starting to date, could be a source of sadness or resentment, but most people didn't dwell on these lost friendships. Rather, while wishing it could have been otherwise, they accepted that some of their friends could not help them with their losses or with their choice to move into other loving relationships.

The problems that were most troubling to our group were those that involved their children. While some individuals and couples chose just to let time work things out—or not—others took a more active role in trying to resolve issues pertaining to their children.

Though people have different styles and approaches to handling problems, there were some important steps that led to resolution, or best efforts toward resolution, in our group. First, the couple had to agree that there was a problem and agree upon the nature of the problem. This involved being able and willing to recognize that one's own child or children or other family members were upset by some aspect of the couple's coming together. Often this meant recognizing troubled or inappropriate behavior of some kind—not always an easy thing to do.

Next, the couple had to agree on a strategy for addressing the issue. Just as with blended families after divorce, the couple had to be unified in their approach if others were to take them seriously. For some couples or individuals, avoiding having a strategy was a barrier to problem solving.

It is advantageous to consider carefully who would be the best person to approach the troubled friend or family member and what might be the best way to do so. Typically, these were emotionally charged situations in which understanding and resolution were the goals. Often it was best for the member of the couple who was closest to the troubled person to take the lead. We tend to trust a person we know well rather than a relative stranger, especially when confronting sensitive and personal issues. On the other hand, a new love, as a less entangled party, might be able to bring a fresh perspective to resolution.

Not surprisingly, respectful communication was crucial to problem solving. It's easy to think we can deduce other people's feelings from their behavior or assume we know the source of the feelings we ascribe to them. These are foolish assumptions and can lead to needless discord. Being open to hearing what the reality is for others, even if we might not want to hear it, is essential to finding a solution. Perhaps some people feared that if they listened to a child's objection, the new relationship would be jeopardized, as the only solution would be to discontinue the new relationship. Other people clearly wanted to avoid any kind of frank discussion about difficult matters and chose to let things slide. Honest communication and emotional courage were valuable in alleviating problems with family members and friends.

The couples in our group did not waver in their intentions to pursue their new love relationships despite the challenges they encountered. Facing the problems together created opportunities to be honest with one another and to widen the circle of acceptance of the partners as a couple. Every challenge-opportunity, therefore, was a chance for increased interpersonal intimacy—with each other and with others.

Sometimes taking action and discovering what was troubling a friend or family member didn't lead to resolution. In these instances, friendships were lost or family relationships became strained or distant. More time was often needed for people outside the couple to grieve and have more time to adjust to the idea that the widow or widower was pursuing new love. There was little the couple could do in these instances but be patient and not expect or try to force others to be as happy as they were.

There is an old saying: "Time heals all wounds." That may be so if you skin your knee, but when wounded by significant life events, people's tender feelings are not so easily mended. Time may help, but the events that occur are most healing. Margaret and Milton found that minimizing family gatherings while his family was still actively grieving his wife's death was helpful in the family's eventual acceptance of the new relationship. They also agreed initially to minimize their affectionate behavior toward one another in his family's presence. They hoped to convey their respect for the family's grief and not unduly display their happiness to those who were struggling. Jody and Tony found that his children's attitudes toward her grew much more positive after they witnessed her caring for him after a major surgery. Seeing Jody's devotion to their father alleviated their doubts about her. Time alone would have shifted things much more slowly.

New partners play a major role in facilitating acceptance by family and friends. Though it may be difficult to do, it's important nonetheless to resist taking the objections and opposition to the new relationship personally. We found from our group that usually the new person, per se, was not the problem. It was the fact that the widow or widower had found a new relationship. However, as would be expected, there were times when there was not an affinty between a new partner and the children or friends of the widow or widower, just as there is not always an affinity between members of biologically-related family members. It was also important for new partners to be patient as friends and family members adjusted to the idea that a widow or widower was moving on to a new love. Too much contact could increase resistance, yet having some contact promoted the couple as the "new normal."

The acknowledgment by a new partner of the deceased person, either overtly or covertly, sent a strong message that he or she recognized the value of the earlier relationship and the importance of the person who had died. Talking or inquiring about that person or being interested in family photos and family stories conveyed the new love's comfort with the earlier relationship. In turn, this comfort helped promote acceptance of the new relationship by family and friends.

Chapter 9

Solidifying Relationships

Our relationship grew quickly and smoothly. We shared a love of nature, were both content with ourselves, and homebodies, not concerned with money and material things.

—Kate

We were interested in what factors solidified our couples' new relationships following their initial assessment of, interest in, and attraction to one another. We asked them what fueled their pursuit of each other and might still be part of their relationship. We discovered that in many respects these relationships were enhanced in ways common to other relationships in which a death has not occurred previously. We found this reassuring and comforting. Even though there is at some level the presence of the person who has died, people could focus on one another and on their partnership in typical ways.

Shared Interests

The most common factor in facilitating an ongoing relationship was shared interests. Over half of our couples said that enjoyment of participation in activities together created a critical bond between them. For some, it was a common interest that had brought them together in the first place. Others developed new interests because of the new partner. The interests varied widely from sedate and contemplative, such as meditation, reading, watching movies, and listening to music, to active, including gardening, dancing, traveling, cooking, hiking, biking, singing, riding motorcycles, boating, spending time with family, and volunteering in community and church activities. It was clear that the new couples we talked with were people actively engaged in life, and sharing their experiences with a partner seemed to enrich their individual experiences. Of course, these were also people who reported having been lonely earlier and desiring companionship.

Though one of the oldest couples in our group, Lorraine and Patrick were in good health. For many years, each had tended to a chronically ill spouse whose limitations precluded shared physical activity. Lorraine told us:

> *We met in a hiking group. Hiking and traveling together are great joys in our relationship, especially because neither of our earlier spouses was well enough to do these things with us.*

Lorraine was pleased that after she and Patrick had gotten together she had made a sports fan of him and also introduced him to playing tennis. Patrick was in his eighties when he acquired these new interests—so you *can* teach an old guy new tricks.

Similarly, Cynthia and Scott met in a dance class, and their shared love of dancing not only brought them together but also became an activity they shared several times a week. While Sandra and

Paul liked hiking and dancing, they also found pleasure in praying together and in reading aloud to one another regularly.

In addition to shared activities, several couples mentioned that having separate activities was also important; they found value in having some time apart to engage in individually meaningful pursuits. Sharing these experiences later in conversation enlivened their relationships. The balance of independent and shared activities varied significantly in our group. The desire to maintain some separateness was very important to some, far less so for others; the critical factor was agreeing on how much shared and independent time each person would pursue.

Communication

The ability to communicate with one another was the second most frequent factor our couples mentioned as enhancing their relationships. It was an essential component for couples with whom challenges could have derailed the relationship. Being able to discuss difficult situations honestly served to create understanding between the partners and helped them face problem situations together. Dealing with family members who were not supportive of the relationships encouraged couples to share hurt and troubled feelings, to talk about the hard stuff, and chart a course together. For example, as discussed earlier, being able to talk about challenges was essential to Laura and Brian, as Laura's young daughter resisted Brian's presence in their lives. Through talking, this couple worked on their mutual goal of helping Laura's daughter accept Brian, and found that their persistent communication paved the way to their success.

Couples also found solace in talking together about the events and feelings surrounding the death of one or both of their spouses. For the surviving partner, being able to talk about such a culturally taboo subject with another person promoted feelings of intimacy and love. Further, finding a new potential partner who could listen, ask questions about, and understand death and grieving fostered emotional closeness in the couple. Tom, a very private person, had spoken virtually not at all about Christine's prolonged illness and death. When he and Sally began seeing each other, Sally encouraged him to talk to her about these experiences. While reluctant at first, ultimately Tom found talking about this difficult time in his life was therapeutic and a significant factor in his love for Sally.

The importance of communication was not restricted to difficulties. Our couples found pleasure in being able to talk to their new partners about anything that was of interest. We often heard the word "openness" to describe not only being able to talk but also being willing to be honest and vulnerable. Honesty in communication was a highly valued attribute.

During the interviews, we observed firsthand the quality of communication, both verbal and nonverbal, with these couples. We inquired about many emotionally laden events in their lives. It was common to see people lock eyes with each other while recounting a difficult or particularly joyous time;

to convey empathy and support with words or gestures; to laugh together or supply words the other had temporarily forgotten. The partners' ability to be candid when discussing difficult situations revealed a significant level of honesty in their relationships.

Trust—Morality—Core Values

Another set of qualities that enhanced these relationships seemed to be related to honesty more broadly. Participants described their relationships using words such as "comfortable," "safe," and "compatible," while also reporting on the trust and respect they felt for each other. Such descriptions suggest a foundation of shared values in the relationship and a sense of harmony and emotional safety. Because of these underlying shared values, the couples trusted their partners (it's easier to trust someone who shares your values), counting on them to be honest, loyal, and cognizant of their feelings.

The importance of these personal characteristics may reflect, in part, the fact that these individuals, whether widowed or new partner, had experienced previous relationships. In addition, most were older and likely wiser people. What they had learned about themselves, what they sought in a new partner, and all that had gone before had influenced what they now considered important in life. Marilyn and Stuart had each had long prior marriages that ended with the death of a spouse. They told us:

> *Life is about what is important to us. Material things have lost their importance. We know who we are and what we like to do. We enjoy every day and don't get upset about small stuff.*

Our couples gave us the impression that they were intent on making their relationships a lasting positive force in their lives: they were "all in." To some degree, this positive, committed attitude likely reflects the nature of intentional relationships formed past middle age. The increasing awareness of one's mortality combined with accumulated life lessons can prompt a conscious effort to make the most of remaining years—to make choices, large and small, that enhance the quality of life. Certainly experiencing a death of a spouse can be the impetus for reassessing what is truly of importance.

Physical Attraction

Physical appearance and passion also played a part in these new relationships, not just in bringing people together but also in fostering deepening relationships. About twenty percent of the people we talked with said that the way a person looked was a factor in their feeling attracted. This was true for both men and women; however, personal qualities were definitely more important than appearance both in attracting and in sustaining relationships. For a lot of couples, becoming sexually active again was an invigorating discovery. Many said they felt like teenagers. Finding sexual pleasure in addition to a loving relationship was like a bonus prize. Several people mentioned they were reassured by a new potential sexual partner's willingness to be tested for HIV, a recent reality for people wanting to be sexually active.

Chapter 10

Where Are the Deceased Now?

Peter is not a ghost—he is a fact.

—Andrew

Whenever couples who've had previous relationships become committed to each other, the reality of the previous relationships and the people who were in them come along in some form or another. Unlike previous relationships that end in divorce, most relationships that end with the death of a partner are not desired. There are exceptions, of course, and a few of our widowed persons were relieved to be out of troubled relationships, but the vast majority of the people we talked with valued their earlier relationships. How, then, do people incorporate, make room for, or remember the deceased persons in the context of new relationships?

Eleanor told us:

The person dies but not the relationship.

Doug said:

I gave many of her belongings away because I didn't need them. She lives inside of me for the rest of my life.

Trina said of her deceased husband:

He and I are comfortable with each other.

Each of these individuals found a way of being in relationship with the deceased, whether widowed or partnering with a widowed person. Each expressed how important the earlier person and relationship had been and continued to be.

The most common presence of those who had died was in conversation about them. Being able to talk about the deceased early in new relationships aided grieving and was important in fostering relationships. Couples talked about how easy it was, now that they were partners, to include the deceased in their conversations—not dwelling on the deceased or the past but not having to hide the fact that many years had been spent with another person, often very happily. Given that the average number of years our widows and widowers had been together prior to their spouses' deaths was more than twenty-seven, it's no surprise that they continue to talk about these earlier significant relationships. To avoid doing so could be damaging to the current relationship.

Hannah and John had each been widowed after a long relationship, and had been together for ten years. They still talked about their spouses regularly. Both Ann and Brad were also widowed, and appreciated that they could talk openly and easily about their earlier spouses. Ann told us:

For us, talking about our earlier spouses was part of knowing them and honoring them.

Further, Ann and Brad each still had children at home, and for these children, keeping memories alive of parents now gone was important. Many couples expressed how happy they were that they could acknowledge the deceased in their new relationships. And many new partners spoke warmly of the departed, aware that this person had been important in shaping their partner into the person they now loved. Quite a few even said they wished they'd known the deceased because they thought he or she was a wonderful person. Hannah and John, both of whom had been widowed, occasionally called each other by their deceased spouses' names and felt that was only to be expected after very long earlier relationships. Marion told us:

When Joe calls me by his deceased wife's name,
I feel honored because I know that he loved her
very much.

The comfortable inclusion of the deceased partners in these new relationships was possible largely because, though present, they were not enshrined on altars by the surviving partners. Memories were cherished as a reality of former lives, not as ideals that were now unattainable. This resulted in the ability of new partners to recognize the reality of the loss and accept in the new relationship the place of the person who had died.

One couple who was an exception to this pattern was Lorraine and Patrick. Surprisingly, they had experienced the longest two previous relationships. Patrick moved into Lorraine's house after they were married, a house he said, "with a ghost." He felt it was important to appreciate the present and not dwell on memories of the past. Lorraine was more likely to keep her feelings inside. The result is that they don't talk much about their deceased spouses. Perhaps their age, in addition to their personalities, plays a role. As people in their eighties, they are aware that their time together is limited, though both are quite healthy now. The desire to savor their time together, to enjoy the activities they share and to live in the present is perhaps so strong that they feel guarded about bringing up the past.

After such a long prior relationship it's hard to imagine how a person could not refer to earlier life events that included the deceased spouse; however, Cynthia, whose first husband had been an irresponsible alcoholic and left her with enormous debts, also did not talk about him with her new partner. There had been too many troubled years with him, and she didn't want to bring that negative energy into her wonderful and positive relationship with Scott.

Ties with Extended Family

Another way of including a deceased person in a new relationship was through continuing association with his or her extended family—parents, brothers, sisters. Though we didn't ask specifically about these relationships, we did learn about them from some of our couples. There was wide variability in the maintenance of relationships with the extended family of a deceased partner, and not all of these extended family relationships had been robust before the death. Some ongoing connections were driven largely by obligation, while others were driven by the strength of positive relationships that existed prior to the death of a partner. Ann had a very close relationship with Collin's family who felt more like family to her than her biological family. When her relationship with Brad became serious, Collin's family was worried that Ann would "give them up." She did not, and in fact they attended her wedding to Brad.

Those people who were widowed when they still had young children were likely to foster relationships at least with the children's grandparents. Some of these relationships remained strong over the years. Complications and resentments could erupt when a new couple with young children married and the new "father" adopted the children. This was the situation for Bonnie, whose young son was an infant when Ned died, and was just under three years old when she married Peter. Bonnie had maintained a relationship with Ned's parents, and it was understandably very difficult for these grandparents when Peter adopted this child and changed his last name. There was a further complication when Bonnie and Peter had other children whom the grandparents at first did not acknowledge. With effort, hurt feelings on both sides were eventually mended and relationships were maintained over time.

Alan was like other widows and widowers who did not maintain regular contact with a deceased spouse's family but welcomed connection that occurred spontaneously. Of course, if relatives lived in other parts of the country, it was easier to let relationships drift away. When relationships with extended family had been difficult prior to a death, there was little incentive or motivation to continue them. One widow, Trina, maintained a relationship with Nate's elderly parents after his death, even though they were critical and demanding of her. She persevered because of her love for Nate and her belief that he would want her to be helpful to them in their declining years, particularly as he was unable to.

Belongings

What did the survivors do with their deceased partners' belongings? Clothing, jewelry, furniture, files, tools, and other ordinary and treasured items must be dealt with eventually. People wrestled with these decisions. Disposing of belongings was understandably difficult, given considerable thought, and typically not accomplished immediately after the death. It's one of the concrete actions that remind us in a most salient way that the deceased person is gone and will no longer need these belongings. It also involves actions that signal that the surviving partner is severing another of the ties to that person—a step in the process of letting go. Decisions about possessions of the deceased were often made before a widow or widower contemplated a new partnership, and for others it was because of a new partnership.

Clothing, jewelry, and tools were most often given to friends or family who would find them meaningful or were given to charities. Widows and widowers also kept items they valued. It was not unusual for widows to wear jewelry and clothing that held particular memories of the deceased. Furniture was often kept and incorporated into the blending of households. Some couples felt comfortable displaying photos that included the person who had died, while others did not. A few couples chose to display photos of family groups that included the deceased person but not photos of only the earlier married couple. A few couples had been together long enough that all their displayed photos were of their own lives.

Having to make decisions about the belongings of the deceased was particularly critical for those couples who were living in the house where the deceased person had lived. Paul moved into the house that Sandra and Alden had lived in after he and Sandra were married. Paul told of his experience:

> *I was appreciative of Sandra, who led the way in "merging and purging." I also completed projects that Alden had begun but had not been able to finish. In that way, I contributed to making Sandra's home into our home. She helped me to feel comfortable there and did not keep objects as idols.*

Tom and Sally approached the situation similarly when Sally moved into the house that Tom and Christine had lived in for many years. Sally told us:

> *We removed some of the most personal of Christine's possessions, moved in some of my furniture, and painted walls with colors that we chose together. My new gardens also helped me to stake out a space and feel the place was now ours.*

Kate was in the process of refurbishing the house she and Bill lived in after his wife's death. Kate still didn't feel ownership in it but seemed confident that she would. The willingness of a widow or widower to alter things in a house where the previous couple had lived indicated an investment in and commitment to the new relationship. In turn, this commitment prevented the new partner from feeling like a stranger in his or her own house, a situation that could significantly erode the relationship.

Wedding Rings

Engagement and wedding rings are powerful symbols of commitment. To our couples, they are powerful symbols of the previous relationships. The various ways that widows and widowers chose to handle them was another way that individuality was evident.

Some widows and widowers took off their wedding rings right after the death or before they entered the dating world. Others took them off just prior to becoming seriously involved or asking the new love to marry. Several women moved their engagement rings from their left to their right hands and removed their wedding rings. Both men and women had the stones from engagement rings reconfigured into new rings or necklaces or wore them on chains. Widows and widowers also gave rings to their children or often stored them in special places, waiting for the right solution to come to them.

Some time after he asked me to marry him, I asked Alan, who was still wearing his wedding band from Susan, "How are you going to be married to both Susan and me?"

Alan claimed he hadn't even thought about the fact that he was still wearing the ring that symbolized their union, but I had noticed and was waiting to see what would happen. Removing it was a tangible sign that Alan was really ready to be married to someone else—me. He did take it off one day at a special place he and Susan had loved, and threw it into the sea where some of her ashes had been scattered.

Chapter 11

Surprises

Scott and I are intentionally happy. We both had pent-up joy for life waiting to be expressed, and we appreciate not only our own joy but each other's joy too.

—Cynthia

The couples who shared their stories with us did so with great sincerity, interest, and often exuberance. These were people who were delighted to have found each other and expressed their gratitude, especially when we asked what had surprised them about their relationships.

The depth of joy and fun they had found together was a surprise for many of our couples. John said he never thought he could be so happy, particularly inasmuch as his earlier relationship with Louise had been stressful and unhappy. His new wife, Hannah, a widow, said:

We each have a good sense of humor. We have fun every day.

For many, the delight of the new relationship was combined with a sense of being lucky to have another wonderful relationship. Bill said he felt his whole life had been lucky, and he was lucky again to have another wonderful wife in Kate. Lorraine and Patrick felt it was a miracle that they had met and found each other, particularly because they were in their eighties. Widowed at the age of sixty-five, Marilyn never expected to have another relationship and told us:

> *Mitch and I had such a wonderful marriage before he died. I expected to spend my remaining days and years enjoying my children and grandchildren. Then Stuart and I started spending time together because we had each lost a spouse. We fell in love. Life is now an unexpected pleasure.*

Ella and Hank, who met through an online dating site, were amazed that of the tens of thousands of people looking for dates or partners, they actually found each other; in fact, Hank was the first man Ella contacted. Others also expressed the opinion that finding each other was a miracle, the result of divine intervention or a gift from God.

Some were surprised that they could love so deeply again. Patrick felt it was miraculous that he found Lorraine, a person he loves deeply. After having such a deep love for Richard and being devastated by his death, Ella had the same surprise about the depth of her love for Hank. Hannah and Trina each felt surprised that another man could love them as deeply as their first husbands had.

Finding joy after the sadness of loss could also be a surprise. Laura said:

> *Life had been gray for a long time before I finally agreed to see Brian and let myself consider another relationship.*

Maria had been surprised that:

...after being so lonely and sad following Grant's sudden death, I could have strong loving feelings again—for Nate.

Stuart had also been devastated by Ellen's sudden death:

With Marilyn I was able to overcome my feelings of loss and emptiness and feel complete again.

Peggy expressed the following about her new relationship:

Kirk feels like a soul mate. Our love is particularly poignant because we are in the autumn of our lives. Because we are in our sixties we don't have the long horizon of the young, and want to make the most of the time we do have together.

Lorraine and Patrick were married in their eighties. They married the day before her granddaughter's wedding, when the whole family was gathered for that celebration. Lorraine said:

My family was happy that I had found a new love after caretaking Christopher for so many years. Just after the ceremony, I looked at the smiling faces of my children and their spouses and my grandchildren. It was the nicest feeling I've ever had!

Gaining an expanded family was also a surprising benefit. People were happy to have new relationships with brothers- and sisters-in-law, nieces and nephews, and children who were wonderful additions to life.

Lest anyone believe that passion and sex are exclusively a part of the joy of relationships in the younger set, our couples told us otherwise and were often surprised themselves. Karen and Paul talked about the emotional, physical, and spiritual depth of their sexual intimacy. Ann and Brad echoed those feelings, relishing the intensity of their sexual relationship. Hannah was surprised that after years without a sexual relationship, due to her first husband's neurological illness, she found so much joy in sex with John. Peggy felt a reawakening in her sexual life with Kirk and loved the feelings of youthfulness and vitality that came with it.

Chapter 12

Wisdom

No one can fill the void. Appreciate the new person for who he or she is.

—Joe

We asked our couples what wisdom they would pass along to others if they could, based on their experiences. First, from the voices of widowed people whose next marriages didn't last. Maria felt that she didn't take enough time to assess her feelings about Nate after they started dating. He was good to her and her young child and helped her hold her grief. She had strong feelings for him, but didn't listen enough to her own warning voices, as she wanted so much for her young child to have a father. There were signs of his untreated depression, unpredictable irritability toward her, and difficulty in committing to marriage even though they had been functioning as a family. They did have some good years together, but eventually her misgivings about him came to the forefront and their marriage dissolved.

Some time after Lana's death, Trent felt desperate to be with someone. He and Diane had lots of fun together, but he felt pressured by her to marry, and let himself drift into marriage more than make a conscious decision. He thinks he should have paid more attention to his doubts and listened to his gut, which was telling him that the relationship wasn't right for him in the long run. It would have saved a lot of pain.

We heard a different experience from the couples who were together, whose relationships were strong and satisfying. We have no idea whether they represent the broad spectrum of experiences widows and widowers have, only that this is what our group experienced. Having a new relationship is not the path for every widow or widower; in fact, seeking a new relationship isn't common for most widowed people, and not everyone in a new relationship will find the satisfaction these couples found. Still, it's enlightening to see what they learned. They advise others to:

- Keep a sense of humor.
- Don't compare your new partner with the deceased partner; appreciate each for his or her own qualities.
- Make room for the deceased partner in your new life.
- Respect the situation of a grieving person. There is complexity with family and friends in integrating a new person.
- Communicate openly.
- Let unimportant things go.
- Get involved in your community and keep a larger life perspective—the loss is painful but not the end of the world.
- Be courageous—no matter how devastated you may be, things change.
- Live in the present.

Of all the people who spoke with us, Bonnie, whose husband died when they were in their twenties, had the longest view of this process. She and Peter have been married for over forty years now. She said:

> *Don't hang on to the past, be in the present. The past relationship is like a good book—finish it, close it, look at it when you want to, but don't carry it around. Don't disrespect either your deceased partner or your new partner by carrying it around.*

Letting oneself grieve, letting go, knowing oneself, and being satisfied with oneself were factors mentioned by many in our group as important in being ready to have another partner. Sharon found:

> *Learning to live with the loss, not die because of it, helped me heal.*

Letting others help with grieving—therapists, friends, support groups—facilitated letting go and knowing oneself. But, as Sharon cautioned:

> *You can't expect others to make it okay for you. You have to do it yourself.*

Doug and Cornelia borrowed Doug's therapist's analogy:

> *Grief is like standing in a wave. There's no way out of it; you have to go into it. By doing so, you open up the possibility for something new coming into your life.*

These couples were thriving in their relationships, so it's not surprising that the most common lesson expressed was: *Go for it!* This attitude brought joy and fulfillment to life. Hannah said:

"Life goes on—live it. Eat dessert first, use the good china, don't put plastic on your furniture. Be open to what life brings."

Peggy felt:

The best way to honor Stan's memory is for me to be happy and love others. If that was not a new love then love of the beauty of life.

Ella simply said:

Jump! Otherwise next year you'll still be sitting there all alone.

To Eleanor, however, the abundance of love was most meaningful:

Although the love with a new partner may be different from the love experienced before, it is wonderful to have loving feelings in your life, not to have to cut off that abundant part of yourself. For me, life is more meaningful when shared.

And Cornelia and Doug offered this wisdom:

Falling in love again doesn't diminish the love you had for your deceased partner or the grief you feel. They live side by side.

In a poignant *New York Times* article entitled "Till Death Do Us Part, And Then Some: Ghosts Keep a Marriage Floating," June Bingham writes about her and her second husband's experiences, being married for almost twenty years after the deaths of their first spouses. Like some of the people in our group, June and her new husband, Bob, were approaching seventy when they remarried after long first marriages. Also like many in our group, at least one family member was not happy about this remarriage, feeling that the deceased person was being replaced. It is clear from the people we talked with that a new partner is not intended to, or even could, replace the deceased partner. June found that although she had forever lost a person she loved and could not replace, she could re-establish a marital relationship, a lifestyle she valued. And June knew what so many people also told us—that grieving and falling in love are not mutually exclusive. They can occur in concert with one another.

June also said that when she and Bob stood at the altar to be married, they were joined by the spirits of their former spouses, Jonathan and Dorothy, and that still, after all those years, they talk about them regularly. Every Valentine's Day June selects the right card for Bob, and without thinking, looks for the right card for Jonathan.

The generous people in our group taught us many things about the fragility, vulnerability, courage, and love human beings are capable of. From them we learned:

- We have a capacity, often unknown to us, to live with tremendous loss that we think could permanently crush us.
- We have a capacity, often a drive, to move through the loss to find meaning in life again.
- Not all people are devastated by the death of a spouse.
- We have an abundant capacity to love.
- Love can blossom and persist even in the presence of loss and grief.
- Love is expansive: we can have more than one big love.
- New love can visit and thrive at any age.

Chapter 13

Parting Words

What a journey—this business of the heart: the joy of falling in love, the heartbreak of losing a love, the elation of falling in love again. The cycle goes on for the couples who talked with us. Unless they happen to die together, one member of each of our couples is destined to be widowed in the future. Of our couples, we know that three have already experienced another death. In two cases, it was wives who succumbed to cancers and one husband who died of natural causes. Thus two widowers and one widow are widowed again.

Widows and Widowers in the United States

What is known in general about the life patterns of widows and widowers? Women are much more likely to be widowed than men, as the life expectancy for women is greater than that for men. Further, men are more likely to marry younger women, who will outlive them, than women are to marry younger men. Of the close to one million people who are widowed yearly in the United States, approximately two thirds are women. The total number of widows (not currently married) of any age is more than four times greater than the number of widowers (US Census Bureau, 2009, 2012).

One factor that influences whether widows and widowers will remarry is the potential number of partners. Here, men have a distinct advantage. The disparity between the number of women and the number of men at various ages increases over time substantially. For example, according to the DHHS (Department of Health and Human Services) Profile of Older Americans data from 2009, for every 100 men in the 65–69 age range, there are 114 women, but for every 100 men over 85 years of age there are 216 women. Only about 2% of widows over 65 years remarry and 20% of widowers.

Thus our group of couples represents a select group of people, the ones who chose to seek and found new loving partners. Perhaps those who told us they felt lucky indeed were. Widows in particular were fortunate, statistically speaking, to find new loving partners.

Another factor influencing remarriage is the desire to do so. Susan Barash, women's issues author, describes the different goals that widows and widowers may have following a spouse's death in her book *Second Wives: the Pitfalls and Rewards of Marrying Widowers and Divorced Men*. Though both men and women may be seeking companionship and security, men are looking to find someone who will help with day-to-day living tasks, keep up social contacts and provide structure to their lives. Women, who may actually find their independence to their liking, may be looking more for romance and, therefore, be less hasty to marry, or they may decide that they don't want another partner and the caretaking responsibilities that come with a partner.

Sociologist Eric Klinenberg, in his book, *Going Solo: The Extraordinary Rise and Surprising Appeal of Living Alone,* found women may be happy to be "liberated from the unrecognized, unappreciated and unrewarded responsibilities… as homemakers and caretakers" (p. 89).

In fact, there has been an explosion of both men and women living alone in the past sixty years or so in the United States, not exclusively widows or widowers or the elderly. Klinenberg covers the topic in depth in *Going Solo.* In 1950, 9% of U.S. households were headed by single adults; at present 28% of households are headed by single adults—a threefold increase. The majority of adults in the U.S. are single. There was also a spectacular increase in the 20th century in the number of widowed persons over sixty-five living alone—from 10 percent of that group in 1900 to 62% of the group in 2000.

Klinenberg considers many factors that account for this major demographic shift: the rising status of women and their economic independence; the focus on careers rather than marriage and children in younger people; benefits of Social Security and other social programs such as Medicare for those over sixty-five; the rapidly evolving electronic social networks that connect people remotely rather than requiring face-to-face contact; the decline of the attitude that singles are those unfortunate ones no one wanted; and the rise of the belief in the potency of the individual. Still he discusses two major advantages of having a partner: the "small intimacies" that characterize couples living together and the large financial benefits.

New Loves: Not for Everyone

In *Epilogue: A Memoir,* author Anne Roiphe tells of the conflicted and ambivalent path she took to her decision not to pursue another romantic relationship after the death of her husband. Her path considers far more than caretaking responsibilities. Roiphe gives a rich personal description of the enticements to starting over, companionship being at the heart—someone with whom to share meals, movies, her bed, grandchildren, friends, and travels; someone to talk with at the end of the day; someone to combat the loneliness she feels when her partner is no longer there. She asks:

> *Is this the thing about being alone that I must get used to—I am not here if no one sees or hears me. Like the proverbial tree in the forest I neither fall nor stand unobserved"* (p. 14).

Responding to an ad that her adult daughters placed in a newspaper, her own foray into Match. com, and matchmaking efforts of friends and family, Roiphe recounts experiences with a variety of potential partners. We learn of her reasons for deciding, quickly or not so quickly, against each one. Her commitment to the pursuit is genuine, filled with compassion, humor, and attempts to overlook signs of obvious mismatches, and in the end she decides the pursuit is not for her. She concludes:

> *I do not have my soul mate and most likely will never have another but I will be fine. I can read. I can think. I can work. I can see friends. I can*

watch my grandchildren grow. I can walk in the park and I can listen to music and I can argue politics…. I will make new friends in unexpected places. I will take a trip somewhere I have always wanted to go (p. 213–4).

Roiphe reminds us that having a new love is not for everyone and that life can be meaningful without a new partner, even though partnership has been a significant, meaningful part of an earlier time in life.

Sociology researcher Deborah Carr reports a more scientific examination of dating and remarriage in the *Journal of Marriage and Family*. Using data gathered from the "Changing Lives of Older Couples" (CLOC) study, she assessed widows' and widowers' desire to remarry, interest in dating, and current dating at six months and eighteen months after a spouse's death. Couples were initially interviewed when both were living and the husband's age was at least sixty-five years. Carr found that about 25% of widowers and about 20% of widows expressed a desire to remarry sometime in the future at either six or eighteen months after the death.

There was a bigger gender gap for interest in dating. At the six-month interview almost three times as many widowers as widows wanted to date (17% vs. 6%), and at eighteen months the difference had shrunk a little and many more widowed expressed an interest in dating (widowers 37%, widows 15%). People who were actually dating also showed a wide gender difference. At six months, 15% of widowers were dating and less than 1% of widows, and at eighteen months 23% of widowers and 9% of widows. Further, by the eighteen-month interview, none of the widowed had remarried. If we safely assume that dating precedes marriage, these data are consistent with the DHHS data that fewer widows remarry than widowers.

How does our group of widowed compare? Ours is not a random, scientifically gathered sample, and it is not composed exclusively of older couples. We do know that considerably more widowers were dating their new love partners by six months after the deaths of their spouses than widows, but many of our widowers (and widows) had dated other people before they met their new partners, and we don't know how soon after their spouses' deaths that occurred. We also know that over half of our widowed people were interested in dating and looking for relationships, not necessarily marriage, but companionship and love. That is a considerably larger percentage than found in the Carr study, and likely reflects, to some degree, the fact that about half of our group was widowed before reaching age sixty. In addition, as Carr speculates in her study, the CLOC data were obtained from a sample of people who were born prior to the 1920s when the norm was to be married to a lifetime partner. As divorce has become more prevalent, today's widows and widowers are more likely than ever before to have had more than one marital relationship and to feel comfortable with the idea of having more than one serious, close relationship in life.

Similar to the Carr group, a small percentage of our group expressed that their intention in dating was eventually to be married again. Only four widows and one widower told us they were seeking marriage, and of these, three had been widowed as young women. Ultimately, at the time of our interviews, 60 percent of the couples were married, and a few others would have married but for external limiting factors (e.g., loss of Social Security benefits, prohibition of gay marriage), and a few were engaged to be married. On the other hand, five widows and one widower said they had no intention of marrying again but were in loving, committed relationships.

In the end, we all dream and plan but come to know that life is a journey with surprises and detours, both welcome and not. There are many ways of giving and receiving love. There are many people with whom to share our love. As one Jewish prayer says:

> *We do best homage to our dead when we live our lives most fully, even in the shadow of our loss.*

Alan and I hope that whatever path you take, your life will be full. After all, it is the piece of eternity we all have been given.

References

Ashenburg, Katherine. *The Mourner's Dance: What We Do When People Die.* New York: North Point Press, 2002.

Barash, Susan Shapiro. *Second Wives: The Pitfalls and Rewards of Marrying Widows and Divorced Men.* Far Hills, NJ: New Horizon Press, 2000.

Bingham, June. "Till Death Do Us Part, And Then Some: Ghosts Keep a Marriage Floating." *The New York Times:* April 12, 2005.

Bonanno, George A. *The Other Side of Sadness: What the New Science of Bereavement Tells Us About Life After Loss.* New York: Basic Books, 2009.

Campbell, Joseph. *A Joseph Campbell Companion: Reflections on the Art of Living.* Robert Walter, ed. San Anselmo, California: Joseph Campbell Foundation, 2012.

Carr, Deborah. "The Desire to Date and Remarry Among Older Widows and Widowers." *Journal of Marriage and Family,* 2004, Vol. 66, 1051–1068.

Carr, Deborah S., Nesse, Randolph and Wortman, Camille B. (Eds.). *Spousal Bereavement in Late Life.* New York: Springer Publishing Co., 2006.

Department of Health and Human Services. *Profile of Older Americans.* US Census and National Center for Health Statistics/Health Data, 2009.

Elison, Jennifer and Chris McGonigle. *Liberating Losses: When Death Brings Relief.* Cambridge: De Capo Lifelong, 2003.

Harland, Marion and Virginia van de Water. *Marion Harland's Complete Etiquette: A Young People's Guide to Every Social Occasion.* Indianapolis: The Bobbs-Merrill Company, 1914.

Jewish Prayer for High Holydays. From McCracken, Anne and Mary Semel. *A Broken Heart Still Beats After Your Child Dies.* Center City, MN: Hazelden, 1998.

Klinenberg, Eric. *Going Solo: The Extraordinary Rise and Surprising Appeal of Living Alone.* New York: The Penguin Press, 2012.

Kenady, Christine Ratliff. Personal interview, May 2013.

Kübler-Ross, Elisabeth. *On Death and Dying.* New York: Macmillan, 1969.

Moore, Alinde J. and Dorothy C. Stratton. *Resilient Widowers: Older Men Speak for Themselves.* New York: Springer Publishing Co., 2002.

US Census Bureau. American Community Survey, 2009, 2012.

Roiphe, Anne. *Epilogue: A Memoir.* New York: Harper-Collins, 2008.

Van den Hoonaard, Deborah K. *By Himself: The Older Man's Experience of Widowhood.* Toronto: University of Toronto Press, Inc., 2010 (a).

_____. *The Widowed Self: The Older Woman's Journey Through Widowhood.* Waterloo, Ontario: Wilfrid Laurier University Press, 2001. (b)

About the Author

Janice Sargent Wiemeyer was a clinical psychologist in Utah and Washington state until her retirement in 2011 and was on the faculty of the Department of Pediatrics, University of Utah School of Medicine. She and her husband, Alan, live on Orcas Island in Washington State.

Lightning Source UK Ltd.
Milton Keynes UK
UKHW010009050821
388321UK00002B/705